From a Race of Storytellers:

From a Race of Storytellers

Essays on the Ballad Novels
of Sharyn McCrumb

Edited by Kimberley M. Holloway

Mercer University Press
Macon, Georgia

ISBN   0-86554-853-6 (hardback)
        0-86554-893-5 (paperback)

MUP   H590   P261

First Edition.

∞The paper used in this publication meets the minimum requirements
of American National Standard for Information
Sciences—Permanence of Paper for Printed Library Materials, ANSI
Z39.48-1992.

Library of Congress Cataloging-in-Publication Data

CIP data are available from the Library of Congress

Contents

Acknowledgments

In my life there have been many people who have encouraged me to achieve my goals, whether I thought I could or not. Among those people are my family and friends who have always believed this project would be made a reality. Their words of encouragement and advice have helped me to move forward through each phase of this project with more confidence than I sometimes felt.

Of course, this collection of essays would not be possible without Sharyn McCrumb. Reading her work has given me great pleasure over the years. I'm grateful for both the fine novels she writes and for her willingness to help me to put this collection of essays together. She has served not only as the inspiration for all the essay writers in this volume, but she has also served as my guide and my mentor.

And to each of the writers included in this collection I owe a debt of gratitude. Each one of them agreed to take part in this project without hesitation, and their contributions have produced a wonderful body of work on one of Appalachia's finest writers. Truly, without them and their work this collection would also not be possible.

I'd especially like to thank two of my friends, Katie Vande Brake and Cindy Maddux. Katie did more than contribute an essay for this work. She also encouraged me in more ways than I can count. Having just completed the publication process as a first-time author herself, she gave me the benefit of her experience, and for that I can't thank her enough. Cindy shares my passion for books and reading, and we have spent countless hours discussing the books we've read—especially Sharyn's books.

My children, Jennifer Mongold and Stephanie Kidd, are also among the people to whom I am indebted. During the time I spent working on this project, they encouraged me in small ways. Their patience with me while I worked seemed unending; they never questioned the time I spent reading, writing, editing, and traveling to finish the work on this collection of essays.

Reading has always been an important part of my life, and certain members of my family have modeled and encouraged a love of reading for me. My grandmother, Pauline Warwick, is an avid reader, and from her I learned that one can never read too much. My grandfather, Howard Holloway, was probably as much responsible for my love of books as anyone. Even though he passed away when I was very young, he still left me with the legacy of a bookcase full of Little Golden Books. My parents tell me that he bought me at least one every week. Thanks to him, I learned early the joy of being surrounded by reading material.

But, most of all, I'd like to thank my parents, Bob and Gwen Holloway, who have always made me feel that I could accomplish any task that I set my mind to. When I was growing up, they encouraged my love of books and of reading and learning. I am lucky to have had parents who believed in the importance of following one's passion in life and who gave me the best possible home environment in which to do just that.

To everyone who helped me along this journey—thank you!

Introduction

From a Race of Storytellers

Kimberley M. Holloway

There are those who say that storytellers are born and not made. While this may or may not be true, for Sharyn McCrumb, storytelling is in her blood; she "comes from a race of storytellers." As a child she was put to bed with stories—stories from Greek and Roman mythology as well as family tales and legends. Her father told her the stories of the *Iliad* at an age when other children fall asleep to the familiar lines of *Goldilocks and the Three Bears* or a story from a "Little Golden Book." But he also told her of the adventures and escapades of the members of her own family who have inhabited the Tennessee and North Carolina hill country for generations. And her mother added her own stories, tales of the flatland South of her youth. It is not surprising, then, that at the age of seven, when boys and girls dream of being flight attendants or firemen, young Sharyn knew she would tell tales and write stories; she would become a writer. And so she did.

McCrumb's Ballad novels are the result of her desire to tell the stories she knows best—stories of Appalachia. These novels, which include *If Ever I Return, Pretty Peggy-O, The Hangman's Beautiful*

Daughter, She Walks These Hills, The Rosewood Casket, The Ballad of Frankie Silver, and most recently, *The Songcatcher* and *Ghost Riders,* give the reader a glimpse of life in an Appalachia that really exists. Hamelin, Tennesee, is no stereotypical backwoods small town in which the residents are barely recognizable to natives of Appalachia as east Tennesseans. Instead, McCrumb's fictional Wake County is inhabited by some of the most realistic characters found in novels depicting this often-misunderstood region.

However, the characters and the events in Hamelin, Tennessee, are not the main thrust of these novels. Instead, each novel centers on Appalachia itself and is seen through the eyes of characters that mirror the people of Tennessee towns not unlike Erwin or Jonesborough or Johnson City, or any number of other small towns dotting the southern Appalachians. The stories McCrumb relates are as old as the mountains themselves, but these stories are told in the context of a more modern era.

The Ballad novels, then, allow readers to experience the old themes and legends of the mountains, for each of these novels is based on a theme rather than a plot. These themes contain as much variety as the mountains themselves and address many of the larger issues of life in Appalachia: the inevitable effect the past has on the present, the journeys of both the novels' characters and the mountains themselves, the loss of the land to "progress," and the isolation and injustice often suffered by "mountain people."

Mythology plays a key role in these novels as well. Celtic and Native American mythology is clearly evident in these novels, but the legends of the Greeks, Romans, and even the Egyptians are woven within their pages. Bits of mythology like Nora Bonesteel's pet groundhog named Persey, for the mythological Persephone, or the Native American Nunnehi, who live in a magical, mythical "otherworld," fit easily into the stories of Hamelin, Tennessee. For the careful reader, these hidden gems from the mythologies of ancient civilizations make the reading more than worthwhile.

Interspersed with these older and more established myths are the relatively newer myths and legends of the mountainous regions of the southern Appalachians. This mythology, which McCrumb presents to the reader in a modern setting, comes alive through the eyes of characters such as Sheriff Spencer Arrowood, his deputies Joe LeDonne and Martha Ayers, and the town "wise woman," Nora Bonesteel. Through Nora Bonesteel, who first appears in the second Ballad novel the *Hangman's Beautiful Daughter*, McCrumb introduces the reader to the mythological second sight or, as Nora refers to it, the Sight. This ability to see into the future, whether the seer desires to do so or not, is part of the ancient Celtic culture and mythology brought to the Appalachians by Scotch-Irish settlers. Indeed, the mythological past seems ever present in Hamelin, though the town moves steadily forward, propelled by the progress against which many fight.

The relationship between past and present is an all-encompassing theme in *If Ever I Return, Pretty Peggy-O, The Rosewood Casket, The Ballad of Frankie Silver, The Songcatcher,* and *Ghost Riders.* In each of these novels, McCrumb deals with a situation in present day Appalachia that has roots in either the distant or not so distant past. The nation's past in the Vietnam War and Spencer Arrowood's past family life are the cornerstones in *Peggy.* Individuals as well as the entire town are drawn back to the past and must face it in order to move ahead. The past also plays an important role in the *Rosewood Casket* when Randall Stargill dies, leaving his farm in the hands of his sons. Their decision whether to keep the farm or sell it to a developer is placed in direct contrast to a young woman's desperate fight to keep her family farm no matter the personal cost. This novel takes the reader from early Native Americans conquering the land of prehistoric animals to their own loss of that land to white settlers all the way to the present time of the businessmen's and developers' new conquest of the mountains. The importance of the past is also stressed in *Frankie Silver,* the story of the first woman in North Carolina to be hanged for murder. For Spencer Arrowood, the key to the present lies in the facts surrounding a murder over a century old. But without understanding the past, Spencer can never answer the questions he has about a murder committed in his jurisdiction in the present.

In *She Walks These Hills* McCrumb examines the past and the present, but this novel is also concerned with the journeys of not just the inhabitants—past and present—but also the journey of the mountains themselves across both land and sea. The geological journey of the mountains is the foundation upon which McCrumb bases the stories of the journey home of Katie Wyler, a woman kidnapped by Shawnees, and doctoral candidate Jeremy Cobb's quest to recreate her journey. The novel also chronicles the path of a mentally ill convict's journey from the unfamiliar world of his incarceration to the only memory he has—the freedom of the mountains and the love of his wife. Trapped in the past by an illness that has robbed him of his short-term memory, Harm sets out on a journey that crosses the paths of Katie, Jeremy, and the daughter he has not seen since she was a baby. Harm's daughter, too, is on a journey, a journey into her past where she finds a father and a heritage with which she has not yet come to terms.

The theme of the relationship between the people who have always inhabited the mountains and the people who occupy the surrounding flatlands is one that McCrumb addresses in *The Ballad of Frankie Silver*. The questions Spencer Arrowood has concerning the trial, conviction, and impending execution of mountaineer Fate Harkryder for the murder of a young couple on the Appalachian Trail lead him to question an earlier and eerily similar conviction in North Carolina over a century earlier—the trial, conviction, and execution of nineteen-year-old Frankie Silver. Spencer's quest for justice leads him to question the way mountaineers are viewed by those not of the mountains and finally to understand the fundamental issues of life in the Appalachian highlands.

McCrumb's most recent Ballad novels, *The Songcatcher* and *Ghost Riders* continue to focus on the relationship of the past with the present. In *The Songcatcher*, McCrumb traces a fictional ballad, "The Rowan Stave" (written especially for this novel), from its roots in Scotland, across the Atlantic Ocean to America with young Malcolm McCourry, and finally to the highlands of southern Appalachia. The journeys of the ballad and young Malcolm and present-day folk singer Lark McCourry collide with the search for the missing ballad. The past and the present combine in this novel to powerfully illustrate the hold the past retains on us for generations.

However, it is *Ghost Riders* that is the ballad novel most firmly rooted in the past. It explores the effect that the Civil War still has on our country. This novel, like *The Songcatcher*, takes place in both the past and the present, but in this novel, the past seems more a thing to avoid—almost dangerous. McCrumb, in exploring the past's hold on the present, seems to be telling her readers to leave the past in the past and to worry about the present. Populated with historical men and women of the Civil War era, like Zebulon Vance, as well as characters in the present who arc scarching for answers in the past, like Spencer Arrowood, and the Civil War re-enactors, who are unaware of the effect their war games have on the thin line that separates the past from the present, this novel gives the reader a glimpse into the real world of the Civil War in Appalachia.

This volume contains fifteen essays in which the authors delve deeply into McCrumb's novels and discover a wealth of meaning in them. Dr. Linda Mills Woolsey, professor of English at Houghton College, examines the themes of love, loss, and remembrance in *She Walks These Hills* by using the chain of serpentine that provides clues to the Appalachian Mountains' origins in the highlands of Scotland and beyond. And professor emerita of English at East Tennessee State University, Dr. Anne LeCroy, provides an extensive discussion of the mythology found in McCrumb's early novels, especially *The Hangman's Beautiful Daughter* and *If Ever I Return, Pretty Peggy-O*. In "Sharyn McCrumb's Use of Ballads in *If Ever I Return, Pretty Peggy-O*," Dr. Danny Miller, professor of English at Northern Kentucky University, focuses on McCrumb's use of the ballad "Fennario" in *If Ever I Return, Pretty Peggy-O*. Many writers give their characters names with some special added significance, and Scott Crowder-Vaughn, Assistant Director of Upward Bound, writes of the names McCrumb has chosen for her characters in the Ballad novels. Using characters from each novel, Crowder-Vaughn explores the significance and meaning of the names McCrumb uses. Dr. Susan Wittig Albert, a former English professor at the University of California at Berkeley and college administrator who is now a full-time writer, examines the ballad aspect of *She Walks These Hills* and analyzes the structure of the novel as a ballad. Nora Bonesteel and her knowledge of the "old ways" form the basis of Tennessee Technological University Professor Wanda Jared's analysis of the Ballad novels. In her essay, "Melungeons in McCrumb's Fiction," Katherine Vande Brake, professor of English at King College, discusses McCrumb's Melungeon characters, analyzing the role of this controversial race in the literature of the region. Dr. Lana Whited, associate professor of English at Ferrum College, addresses methods teachers can use in teaching *The Ballad of Frankie Silver* as a true story. In an essay exploring gender, class, and regional tradition in McCrumb's novels, Tanya Mitchell, a doctoral student at the Free University of Berlin, addresses the issues women have traditionally faced in Appalachia in light of the representation of women in the Ballad novels. Another essay that focuses on McCrumb's fictional women is by Danny Miller and Nancy Jentsch, Instructor in German and Spanish at Northern Kentucky University. This essay examines the way McCrumb addresses traditional roles and stereotypes of women in the Ballad novels. Finally, Dr. Joyce Compton Brown, professor of English at Gardner-Webb University, considers the theme of the survival of both individuals and communities in light of changes taking place in Appalachian communities. Dr. Brown offers an in-depth look at the changes McCrumb's characters face and their reaction to that change.

Each essay takes a unique look at McCrumb's work in the Ballad series and demonstrates the depth of meaning found in the novels. For the teacher desiring to bring these stories to life for students, these essays present a wide range of interest and interpretation. For the researcher, this collection is the first to bring together a body of scholarship on McCrumb's work into one volume. And for the reader who wishes to move beyond the surface in these novels, these essays are a chance to read what others have, through research and personal interpretation, discovered in their own studies.

In short, the Ballad novels are filled with a bounty of riches waiting to be discovered and mined for their abundant wealth. Certainly these novels can be read merely for the enjoyment of a "good read." But it would be a shame to leave it there, never to plumb the depths that lie beneath the good read. Like the mountains, these novels have depths—and heights—that have yet to be explored. Mythology, the past, journeys, and societal inequities are just a few of the riches waiting to be discovered by readers and students alike of Sharyn McCrumb's work.

Keepers of the Legends

An essay on the influences of family legends and folklore on fiction

Sharyn McCrumb

"All around the water tank, standing in the rain,
A thousand miles away from home, waiting for a train..."

When I was four, I thought that was the saddest story in the world. It was a Jimmie Rodgers tune, I later learned, but I only ever heard it sung *a cappella* by my father in our old Chevrolet on the five-hour drives to visit my grandparents in east Tennessee.

Who was the fellow in the song, I wondered, and how did he get stuck out there on the desolate Texas prairie all alone, so far from the mountains? He seemed to think he was going to make it home all right, but for the duration of the song, he was stranded, and I could never hear it without feeling the sting of tears.

I come from a race of storytellers.

My father's family—the Arrowoods and the McCourys—settled in the Smoky Mountains of western North Carolina in 1790, when the

wilderness was still Indian country. They came from the north of
England and from Scotland, and they seemed to want mountains, land,
and as few neighbors as possible. The first of the McCourys to settle in
America was my great-great-great grandfather Malcolm McCourry, a
Scot who was kidnapped as a child from the island of Islay in the
Hebrides in 1750, and made to serve as a cabin boy on a sailing ship. He
later became an attorney in Morristown, New Jersey; fought with the
Morris Militia in the American Revolution; and finally settled in what is
now Mitchell County, western North Carolina in 1794. Another relative,
an Arrowood killed in the Battle of Waynesville in May 1865, was the
last man to die in the Civil War east of the Mississippi. Yet another
"connection" (we are cousins-in-law through the Howell family) is the
convicted murderess Frankie Silver, the subject of *The Ballad of Frankie
Silver*. Frances Stewart Silver (1813–1833) was the first woman hanged
for murder in the state of North Carolina. I did not discover the family tie
that links us until I began the two years of research prior to writing the
novel. I wasn't surprised, though. Since both our families had been in
Mitchell County for more than two hundred years, and both produced
large numbers of children to intermarry with other families, I knew the
connection had to be there. These same bloodlines link both Frankie
Silver and me to another Appalachian writer, Wilma Dykeman, and also
to the famous bluegrass musician Del McCoury.

The namesake of my character Spencer Arrowood, my paternal
grandfather, worked in the machine shop of the Clinchfield Railroad. He
was present on that September day in 1916 at the railroad yard in Erwin,
Tennessee, when a circus elephant called Mary was hanged for murder:
she had killed her trainer in Kingsport. (I used this last story as a theme
in *She Walks These Hills*, in which an elderly escaped convict is the
object of a manhunt in the Cherokee National Forest. In the novel the
radio disc jockey Hank the Yank, reminds his listeners of that story as a
prayer for mercy for the hunted fugitive.) I grew up listening to my
father's tales of World War II in the Pacific, and to older family stories
of duels and escapades in Model A Fords. With such adventurers in my
background, I grew up seeing the world as a wild and exciting place; the
quiet tales of suburban angst so popular in modern fiction are alien to
me.

Two of my great-grandfathers were circuit preachers in the North Carolina mountains a hundred years ago, riding horseback over the ridges to preach in a different community each week. Perhaps they are an indication of our family's regard for books, our gift of storytelling and public-speaking, and our love of the Appalachian mountains, all traits that I acquired as a child.

I have said that my books are like Appalachian quilts. I take brightly colored scraps of legends, ballads, fragments of rural life, and local tragedy, and I piece them together into a complex whole that tells not only a story, but also a deeper truth about the culture of the mountain South. It is from the family stories, the traditional music, and from my own careful research of the history, folklore, and geography of the region that I gather the squares for these literary quilts.

Storytelling was an art form that I learned early on. When I was a little girl, my father would come in to tell me a bedtime story, which usually began with a phrase like, "Once there was a prince named Paris, whose father was Priam, the king of Troy...." Thus I got the *Iliad* in nightly installments, geared to the level of a four-year-old's understanding. I grew up in a swirl of tales: the classics retold; ballads or country songs, each having a melody, but above all a *plot;* and family stories about Civil War soldiers, train wrecks, and lost silver mines.

My mother contributed stories of her father, sixteen-year old John Burdette Taylor, a private in the 68th North Carolina Rangers (CSA), whose regiment walked in rag-bound boots, following the railroad tracks from Virginia to Fort Fisher, site of a decisive North Carolina battle. All his life he would remember leaving footprints of blood in the snow as he marched. When John Taylor returned home to Carteret County, eastern North Carolina at the end of the war, his mother who was recovering from typhoid, got up out of her sickbed to attend the welcome home party for her son. She died that night.

My father's family fund of Civil War stories involved great-great uncles in western North Carolina who had discovered a silver mine or a valley of ginseng while roaming the hills, trying to escape conscription into one marauding army or the other. There were the two sides of the South embodied in my parents' oral histories: Mother's family represented the flat-land South, steeped in its magnolia myths, replete with Gorham sterling silver and Wedgwood china. My father's kinfolks spoke for the Appalachian South, where the pioneer spirit took root. In their War Between the States, the Cause was somebody else's business, and the war was a deadly struggle between neighbors. I could not belong completely to either of these Souths because I am inextricably a part of both. This duality of my childhood, a sense of having a foot in two cultures, gave me that sense of *otherness* that one often finds in writers: the feeling of being an outsider, observing one's surroundings, and looking even at personal events at one remove.

So much conflict; so much drama; and two sides to everything. Stories, I learned, involved character, and drama, and they always centered around irrevocable events that mattered.

In addition to personal histories set in Appalachia, I was given a sampling of my father's taste in literature: the romantic adventure tales of H. Rider Haggard and Edgar Rice Burroughs, and the frontier stories of Mark Twain and Bret Harte, and the sentimental surprise-ending works of Dickens and O. Henry. Add to that the poetry of Benet, Tennyson, Whittier, and Longfellow. It is no wonder that, years later, when I was ready to be a published writer, I found that I had no aptitude for minimalism, despite studies in the contemporary trends in creative writing at my alma mater UNC Chapel Hill, and later at Virginia Tech, where I received my M.A. in English. I took all the courses in Victorian literature the university offered, and it was there that I found my mentors.

My role model of a successful, important writer became Charles Dickens, not for his style, but for his philosophy. Charles Dickens wrote best sellers in order to change the world. Here's one example: In the mid-nineteenth century child labor laws in Britain were virtually non-existent. Children worked twelve-hour days in factories, were maimed in coalmines, and died of lung disease in their teens from work as chimney sweeps. No one seemed to care. For decades ministers and social reformers wrote earnest pamphlets reeling off the statistics of child mortality, and calling for child-protection laws. These pamphlets were mostly read by people who already agreed with the author; other ministers and social reformers who were working on pamphlets of their own. And nobody did anything to help the children. Then Charles Dickens wrote a book. It was a novel, about a little boy who suffered terribly in the workhouse: *David Copperfield*. Then came *Oliver Twist*, with its grim picture of a child's life on the street in the slums of London. Those books became best-sellers in Great Britain, and within two years of their publication the child labor laws of England were changed. The general public, who had never bothered to read the informative pamphlets, wept for a little boy who existed only in a novel, and as an echo of the author's childhood. People became so outraged at the fate of these fictional children, that they demanded laws protecting child workers. First Dickens had to make people care; then he could persuade them to act. This is what John Gardner later called "moral fiction," and I knew early on that I wanted my words to make a difference. Writing should do more than entertain.

Even the early "mystery" novels that I wrote reflect this sense of purpose, that a good book should have a message. The books featuring forensic anthropologist Elizabeth MacPherson have been described as "Jane Austen with an Attitude" for the way that they blend social issues into the plots. In each of the early novels, the murder is committed by someone who is trying to protect an assumed cultural identity—not for greed, or revenge, or any of the usual motives. Cultural identity, I learned from my dual-culture childhood, is optional. The point of those novels is not to reveal "whodunit," but to satirize a pretentious segment of society: in *Highland Laddie Gone*, for example, the Scottish Wannabes at the Highland Games are lampooned. *If I'd Killed Him When I Met Him* is a synchronically structured meditation on the dysfunctional nature of contemporary relationships: i.e. there is a war going on between men and women these days, and in this book, Elizabeth MacPherson becomes the war correspondent. These satirical novels reflect the culture of my mother's South: the mannered society where appearances and social position matter. The dark and troubled world of the Ballad novels are the other South, drawn on my father's Appalachian heritage.

The idea of being a writer took root early in my consciousness. When I was seven, I announced that I was going to be a writer—even though I had to ask my parents how to spell about every third word of my compositions. My first work was a poem called "The Gypsy's Ghost" written when I was in the second grade. It had the sing-song rhyme of iambic octameter, and the most frightening thing about it to me now is the specter of seeing it in print, but it told a coherent ghost story in verse, and my parents seemed pleased with my efforts, so I persevered. I must have been nine when I heard the Irish song "Danny Boy" for the first time, and while I recognized the urgency and sadness in the song, I could not figure out where Danny was going, and why his father wasn't sure he'd ever seen him again. Unable to get any satisfactory answers on these points from the lyrics, I invented a story to explain the situation in the song. It has to do with a changeling being reclaimed from his human foster parents by the Irish fairies, but it wasn't a bad effort for a nine-year old's imagination. I still think it might be a good children's book.

This attempt to make sense of the inexplicable by making up my own "legend" is still an occasional source of inspiration to my work, most notably in the novel *If Ever I Return, Pretty Peggy-O,* which began as an attempt to answer the question: "I wonder who lives in that house." *That house* is a stately white mansion set amid stately oaks on Highway 264 on the outskirts of Wilson, North Carolina. My parents lived in Greenville, North Carolina, and practically the only way to reach Greenville from points west was to take Highway 264, which meant that I had been driving past that white mansion for nearly twenty years: home for weekends from UNC Chapel Hill, back from my job as a newspaper reporter in Winston-Salem, and later back from the Virginia Blue Ridge, where my husband and I were attending graduate school at Virginia Tech.

In the spring of 1985 I was driving home by myself when I passed the big white house on Highway 264, and I said for at least the two hundredth time: "I wonder who lives in that house." I still don't know who really lives there: it isn't the sort of place that invites drop-in visits from inquisitive strangers. I decided to answer the question with my imagination. "A woman lives in the house," I thought. "She bought the house with her own money. She didn't marry to get the house, and she didn't inherit it. Who is she?" A folksinger. She would have to have made a substantial amount of money to be able to buy the house, but in order to take up residence in a small Southern town, her career would have to be over.

A character began to take shape. This folksinger had attended UNC-Chapel Hill in the 1960s, as I had. She was still young-looking, a trim blonde woman in her early forties, who had once been a minor celebrity in folk music, but her popularity waned with the change in musical trends, so now she has bought the white mansion in the small Southern town, looking for a place to write new songs, so that she can stage a musical comeback, probably in Nashville. "She doesn't know anybody here," I thought.

I had loved folk music when I was in college, and I had grown up listening to my father's mixture of Ernest Tubb and Francis Child, so I began to consider what songs this folksinger character might have recorded. Since I was alone in the car, I could sing my selections as I drove along. After a couple of Peter, Paul, and Mary tunes, I happened to recall an old mountain ballad called *Little Margaret*. I was reminded of it, because I had heard Kentucky poet laureate Jim Wayne Miller sing it in a speech at Virginia Tech only a few weeks earlier. The song is a Child Ballad. It is four centuries old, and it is a ghost story. Little Margaret sees her lover William ride by with his new bride, and she vows to go to his house to say farewell, and then never to see him again. When she appears like a vision in the newlyweds' bed chamber that night, William realizes that he still loves her, and he goes to her father's house, asking to see her: *"Is Little Margaret in the house, or is she in the hall?"* He receives a chilling reply: *"Little Margaret's lying in her cold, black coffin with her face turned to the wall."*

I sang that verse a few times, because some instinct told me that the heart of my story was right there. The owner of the house is a folksinger. She has moved to a small town, where she doesn't know anybody, and one day she receives a postcard in the mail, with one line printed on the back: *"Is Little Margaret in the house, or is she in the hall?"* The folksinger's name is Margaret! The line would terrify her with its implied threat, and she would take the message personally, because her own name was in the line. Having sung the song many times in her career, she knows the next line: *"Little Margaret's lying in her cold, black coffin with her face turned to the wall."* I pictured her calling the local sheriff in a panic, and saying that someone is threatening her life, but the sheriff sees no threat in the line on the postcard. He tells her that the message is simply a prank. I thought: Suppose something or someone close to her is violently destroyed that night. Then she will know that the threat was serious. Then all she can do is wait for the next postcard to come, as she and the sheriff try to find out who is stalking her.

As I drove toward my parents' house, I followed the thread of the plot, so that by the time I reached Greenville, I knew who lived in that house, (which I had mentally relocated to east Tennessee), and I had the seeds of the first Ballad novel *If Ever I Return, Pretty Peggy-O*. That hour of inspiration was followed by several years of hard work, researching the high school reunions of 1960s' graduates, talking to Vietnam veterans, and interviewing law enforcement people, but the idea itself came from an old mountain song.

The theme of *If Ever I Return, Pretty Peggy-O* came from a more modern melody: the Doors' tune *Strange Days Have Tracked Us Down*. I thought: Suppose "strange days" tracked everybody down one summer in an east Tennessee village. For the Baby Boomers it is their twentieth high school reunion, forcing them to come to terms with their shortcomings; for the sheriff and his deputy, it is the memory of Vietnam, which haunts them both but for different reasons; and for Peggy Muryan, the once-famous folksinger, strange days track her down in the form of a stalker who still remembers her days of celebrity. For Appalachia itself, the Strange Days refer to the time when the traditional folkways began to be lost in the onslaught of the modern media culture. Child ballads gave way to the Top 40; quilts featured cartoon character designs; and the distinctiveness of the region began to erode as it was bombarded by outside influences. In each case "Strange Days" meant the 1960s.

Music is a continuous wellspring of creativity for me. When I was writing the subsequent Appalachian Ballad novels, I would make a sound track for each book, before I began the actual process of writing. The cassette tape, dubbed by me from tracks of albums in my extensive collection, would contain songs that I felt were germane to the themes of the book, and sometimes a song that I thought one of the characters might listen to, or a "theme song" for each of the main characters. Generally, the songs I use to focus my thinking do not appear in the novel itself; they are solely for my benefit, although I have thought of providing a "play list" in the epilogue to each book.

The taped sound track for *She Walks These Hills*, for example, is a mixture of Bluegrass, Scottish folk songs, and modern country music. It begins with the Don Williams recording of "Good Old Boys Like Me," a song that captures the character of Sheriff Spencer Arrowood in a few well-chosen lines: *"...Those Williams boys, they still mean a lot to me: Hank and Tennessee."* A "good old boy" who is able to appreciate both Hank Williams and Tennessee Williams has a blend of urbanity and traditionalism that typifies the rural Tennessee sheriff I wanted to create. The music of Deputy Joe LeDonne's is an acid rock tune from the 1960s, "Break on Through to the Other Side." A Vietnam vet, LeDonne listens only to recordings made in the late 1960s and early 1970s: Otis Redding, the Grateful Dead, Kris Kristofferson, Janis Joplin. Other songs on my home-made album for *She Walks These Hills* include: "Jamie Raeburn," a Scots folk song about a convict forced to leave his homeland; the Bluegrass standard "Fox on the Run," both theme tunes for the novel's escaped convict Harm Sorley, as well as "Poor Wayfaring Stranger;" "The Bounty Hunter" written and sung by North Carolina musician Mike Cross; and a selection of hammered dulcimer recordings of traditional Scottish and Irish melodies.

When the cassette tape is finished, I make one copy of it for my car, and another one for my office. Then during the months that I am researching, before I write a word of the book itself, I play the car tape whenever I am driving, so that I can absorb and internalize the sound and the themes of the novel-to-come. I suppose the music serves as both the means of directing my thoughts along the lines of motivation, characterization and theme during the planning phase of the novel, and later for the creation of mood when I am in my study actually working on the book.

The songs I listen to also provide the titles for the Ballad novels. *If Ever I Return, Pretty Peggy-O* is a line from the Joan Baez recording of *Fenario*, a minor key variation of a Scots folk song alternately called the *Bonnie Streets of Fyvie-O;* a line from the chorus of Danny Dill's 1959 folk revival tune the *Long Black Veil* is the source of the title of *She Walks These Hills*, and *The Rosewood Casket* is a late nineteenth century song, most recently popularized by Dolly Parton, Emmy Lou Harris, and Linda Ronstadt on their album *Trio*. As I write this essay the novel I am working on is entitled *The Ballad of Frankie Silver*, after a song attributed to the first woman hanged for murder in North Carolina (in fact Frankie Silver did not write the song; she was almost certainly illiterate). I am also researching (still in the rather desultory fashion of one who is a long way from a plot) the Civil War in the Appalachian mountains, where the conflict was intensely personal, and there was no great Cause to illuminate the suffering. The song that I find myself listening to when I'm reading Appalachian Civil War material is the traditional tune *Rank Strangers*; surely that will be the title of the book, when I finally sit down to write it. I like the play on words, and the idea conveyed by the song that a civil war suddenly turns neighbors into strangers. The faux cowboy ballad *Ghost Riders in the Sky* is also on my Civil War soundtrack-in-progress. So far, I have no inkling as to why it's there.

I find that the more I write, the more fascinated I become with the idea of the past as prologue. I began the fourth Ballad novel, *The Rosewood Casket,* with a quote from Pinero: "I believe the future is simply the past entered through another gate." In order to make sense of the present, I look to incidents in the past, and I like to know where things came from, so that I can understand how they came to be what they are today. This sense of inquiry led me to read books on such diverse subjects as the legends of the Cherokee, mountain botany and ornithology, and the natural history of Appalachia.

In *The Rosewood Casket*, I wanted to talk about the passing of the land from one group to another, as a preface to the modern story of farm families losing their land to the developers in today's Appalachia. The voice of Daniel Boone is central to the novel's message, a reminder that the land inherited by the farm families was once taken from the Cherokee and the Shawnee. The novel begins with Cherokee wise woman Nancy Ward, in the last spring of her life, as she realizes that her people are about to lose the land that she tried so hard to preserve for them. As a reminder of that transience of ownership, in a passage in chapter one of *The Rosewood Casket*, I trace the passing of the land even farther back: to a time at the end of the last Ice Age, twelve thousand years ago.

Appalachia was a very different place at the end of the Ice Age, when the first humans are believed to have arrived in the mountains. The climate of that far-off time was that of central Canada today, too cold to support the oaks and hickories of our modern forests. Appalachia then was a frozen land of spruce and fir tree, but it was home to a wonderful collection of creatures: mastodons, saber-tooth tigers, camels, horses, sloths the size of pick-up trucks, and birds of prey with wingspans of twenty-five feet. The kingdom of ice that was Appalachia in 10,000 BC was their world, and they lost it to the first human settlers of the region, who hunted the beasts to extinction in only a few hundred years. Losing the land is an eternal process, I wanted to say. It seemed fitting to start with these early residents, as a reminder that even the Indians were once interlopers. The theme song for that book was *Will the Circle Be Unbroken?*

A scholarly publication on Appalachian geology provided me with one of the central themes of *She Walks These Hills*, a novel of intertwining journeys, past and present. An elderly convict escapes from the Northeast Correctional Center in Mountain City, Tennessee, and tries to make his way home through the same stretch of wilderness in which a Virginia Tech history professor is re-enacting the eighteenth century journey of a pioneer woman who escaped from captivity with the Shawnee. The climax of the novel is the convergence of all these epic journeys.

From a book by Dr. Kevin Dann, *Traces on the Appalachians: A History of Serpentine in America* (Rutgers University Press, 1988), I learned that the first journey was the journey made by the mountains themselves. A vein of a green mineral called serpentine forms its own subterranean "Appalachian Trail" along the mountains, stretching from north Georgia to the hills of Nova Scotia, where it seems to stop. This same vein of serpentine can be found in the mountains of western Ireland, where it again stretches north into Cornwall, Wales, Scotland, and the Orkneys, finally ending in the Arctic Circle. More than two hundred and fifty million years ago the mountains of Appalachia and the mountains of Great Britain fit together like a jigsaw puzzle. Continental drift pulled them apart at the same time it formed the Atlantic Ocean. I thought this bit of geology was a wonderful metaphor for the journeys reflected in the book, and in a sociological way, it closed the circle: When our pioneer ancestors settled in the mountains because the land looked right, made them feel at home—they were right back in the same mountains they had left to come to America!

Because I do so much research for my novels, and because I like to include so many historical and scientific details in the narrative, people often ask me which comes first: the story or the research. I usually reply by quoting another favorite maxim of mine, one from Louis Pasteur, perhaps an unlikely source of inspiration for a Southern novelist, but his advice is sound for many disciplines. Pasteur said: "Chance favors the prepared mind." Much of my reading is non-fiction, particularly natural history, anthropology, and the sciences. (Once my publisher sent me on a book tour with two other authors and I nearly drove them crazy reading the *Coming Plague* for the entire tour, and intoning ominous bits aloud to them when someone happened to cough.)

My reference shelves fill the all the bookcases in my study, so that I have easy access to trail guides of the Cherokee National Park, field studies of birds and wildflowers, the poetry of Stephen Vincent Benet, the Toe River Valley Heritage book, several hundred volumes of folklore of Britain, and a host of other arcane volumes that I trust libraries do not have in stock.

When I am reading subjects that have nothing to do with the book-in-progress, I am ostensibly reading for pleasure and relaxation, but I am always alert for new ideas. There is no telling when a chance sentence or an unexpected topic will trigger an association, or suggest a subject that can be put to use in one's work. I was reading a medical journal when I discovered Korsakov's Syndrome, the form of brain damage that affected escaped convict Harm Sorley in *She Walks These Hills*. I chose to afflict the character with that mental disorder in order to have him stuck in the past; Harm became a twentieth century version of Don Quixote, forever trapped in a better place and time than Now.

Once I used an idea from folklore that I understood only intuitively, and then later found the confirmation in a volume on Celtic beliefs. The theme for the second Ballad novel *The Hangman's Beautiful Daughter* was the idea of being "betwixt and between:" to be caught in a liminal state between life and death. I found that each of the issues in the novel—(the polluted river, the stillborn child, the country singer forced into retirement, the old woman with the Sight who talks to the dead, the hibernating groundhog; the young suicide who still contacts his grieving sister)—involved someone or something lingering on the threshold between life and death, reaching both ways. My feeling that this theme was integral to the mountain culture was instinctive. After I completed the novel, I found the justification for this theme of liminality in a book discussing Celtic beliefs. In *Ravens and Black Rain: The Story of Highland Second Sight*, Scottish writer Elizabeth Sutherland says:

> Celtic mysteries occurred in tri-states between night and day, in dew that was neither rain nor river, in mistletoe that was not a plant or a tree, in the trance state that was neither sleep nor waking. The Christian sense of duality—good and bad, right and wrong, black and white, body and soul—was unknown to the Druid. The key to Celtic philosophy is the merging of dark and light, natural and supernatural, conscious and unconscious. The *sithean* themselves existed in this tri-state, beings who dwelled between one world and another, creatures who were neither men nor gods.[1]

There it was. The liminality that I kept insisting belonged in the narrative of *The Hangman*'s *Beautiful Daughter* was part of the worldview held by the ancestors of the mountain people for thousands of years. Although I hadn't been sure why I'd felt compelled to put the concept of liminality into the text, now the reason was clear. I was describing people of Scots descent, keeping to the old ways, and this *border* concept is central to their worldview. The scene in the novel in which Nora Bonesteel gathers balm of Gilead plants for making medicine reflected this ancient philosophy. (But I wrote this passage *before* I read Sutherland's work. Is instinctive use of the correct cultural pattern Jungian, or the genius of the unconscious, or was I third from the left over the cauldron in Act One of *Macbeth?*) Anyhow, here is the Celtic belief in liminality as expressed by Appalachian wise woman Nora Bonesteel in chapter ten of *The Hangman's Beautiful Daughter*:

---

[1] Elizabeth Sutherland, *Ravens and Black Rain: The Story of Highland Second Sight* (London: Constable, 1985) 26.

When Nora was a girl, a few of the old women had claimed that balm of Gilead ought to be harvested at dawn or dusk, but these days she dispensed with that part of the ritual. Early mornings and evenings were colder than mid-day, and she was too old to brave a chill for the sake of rough magic. She understood the logic behind the stricture, though. There was a power in the borders of things: in the twilight hours that separated day from night; in rivers that divided lands; in the caves and wells that lay suspended between the earth and the underworld. The ancient holy days had been the divisions between summer and winter, and that border in time created a threshold for other things; that was why ghosts and goblins were thought to roam on Halloween and Beltane. The mountains themselves were a border, Nora thought. They separated the placid coastal plain from the flatland to the west, and there was magic in them.[2]

I read non-fiction incessantly, always trolling for some relevant thought or fact that will add a grace note to the next story. I keep hardbound notebooks for possible future novels, each one labeled with the working title. When I see an article, a quote, or a phrase that might pertain to the subject of this future book, I copy it onto a blank page in the scrapbook. I have discovered through bitter experience that it is much easier to stockpile things you may never use than it is to try to track down an article or a reference several years after you've seen it, when your memory of where it can be found is no longer reliable. The prepared mind saves me much time and energy in the long run, and the background reading that I have done has triggered associations and brought other facets of the story into focus, giving my work a scope and texture that it would not otherwise have.

I read. I study. I interview people who are experts in the subject of the current work. I have hiked the Appalachian Trail with a naturalist,

---

[2] Sharyn McCrumb, *The Hangman's Beautiful Daughter* (New York: Onyx, 1992) 213–14.

and explored country music with Skeeter Davis. I researched wood-working with a master dulcimer-maker, and I have sat in Tennessee's electric chair. I try to write interesting, compelling stories, because I think it is the duty of a fiction writer to entertain, *but*: beyond the reader's concern for the characters, I want there to be an overlay of significance about the issues and the ambiguities that we face in Appalachia today. In my novels I want there to be truth, and an enrichment of the reader's understanding of the mountains and their people. I have been known to warn folks not to read my books with their brains in neutral. Dickens again: "Never be inducted to suppose that I write merely to amuse or without an object." I have a mission.

Appalachia is still trying to live down the stereotypical "backwoods" view of the region presented in the media. I think one of the best ways to combat this negative portrayal is to educate the general reader about the real character of the region, and particularly about the history and origins of Appalachia and its people, both culturally and environmentally. Like Charles Dickens, I think that in order to win hearts and minds, one must reach the greatest possible number of people, and so I am pleased when my novels make the *New York Times* best seller list, because that means that millions of people have been exposed to my point of view. Millions of people watched the *Dukes of Hazzard*: surely the opposite opinion deserves equal time. I am passing along the songs, the stories, and the love of the land to people who did not have a chance to acquire such things from heritage or residence. Perhaps my own theme song ought to be the one Joan Baez recorded on an early album called *One Day at A Time*: "Carry It On."

Carry it on.

"Serpentine Chain:"

Love, Loss, and Remembrance in

She Walks These Hills

Linda Mills Woolsey

In Sharyn McCrumb's *She Walks These Hills* even the trivial and trashy events of contemporary Appalachian life are grounded in the "primordial" reality of ancient hills, ancient beliefs, and fundamental human emotions. Reviewers frequently compare McCrumb's Ballad novels to Appalachian quilts. This novel—with its narrative patterns built of links among a diverse group of characters and interwoven with a rich texture of detail drawn from folklore, history, natural science, and contemporary life—is no exception. If this novel were a quilt, its pattern might be called "serpentine chain." At the heart of the novel's winding narrative of separation and connection lie twin images of the "serpentine chain"—geological and genealogical—that provides kinship, connection, and hope for survival in a world that often seems irrevocably torn apart by greed, hatred, and alienation.

In the midst of a potentially destructive modernization, the mountains themselves provide a central image of enduring kinship. Torn apart ages ago by the forces of continental drift, the Blue Ridge, Great

Smoky, and Unaka mountains are still "kin" to the Alps[1] and the mountains of Scotland.[2] The evidence of this connection is the deposits of a green stone called "serpentine," which appears in mountain chains on both sides of the Atlantic. A number of the characters whose lives are lived out in the midst of these mountains experience a similar separation from kin and from cultural roots, yet regain their connection and rootedness through love, memory, and the struggle for survival in the wilderness of the mountains and of the modern world. One of the novel's key characters, a graduate student of geology named Charlotte Pentland, has substituted geology for genealogy in an attempt to escape her mountain roots as the white trash child, Chalarty Sorley. Yet, as the events of the novel carry her and her mother back to the farm where she lived as a baby, she discovers that she may be "her mother's serpentine chain, entrusted with remembering their past."[3]

The past—forgotten, remembered, persisting, repeated—is inescapable in this novel. The story quilts together layers of time as central characters come to terms with personal, familial, and local past in a world that stretches out beyond these through Thomas Wolfe's "unfound door" into the mysteries of time, space, and existence.[4] Two key figures in the narrative are fugitives who exist in a sort of twilight zone of timelessness and uprootedness. One is sixty-three-year-old Hiram "Harm" Sorley, who has escaped from the prison at Mountain City. Through much of the novel, Sorley is journeying home through the mountains, plagued by Korsakoff's syndrome, which has destroyed his short-term memory, making the present unintelligible. The other is the spirit or ghost of an eighteenth-century fugitive, Katie Wyler. Katie, who escaped her Shawnee captors and traveled three hundred miles through the wilderness, met tragedy on her return home. Like Harm, Katie is "stuck in a certain time," inhabiting an unchanging and timeless world that repeatedly intersects with the constantly changing world of the present.[5]

---

[1] Sharyn McCrumb, *She Walks These Hills* (New York: Signet, 1985) 188.
[2] McCrumb, *Hills*, 301.
[3] McCrumb, *Hills*, 407.
[4] McCrumb, *Hills*, 420.
[5] McCrumb, *Hills*, 64.

Some characters in the story are engaged in a quest to reclaim their own stories and identities, while sympathy and curiosity draw other characters to explore the more distant past of local history and folklore in an effort to discover reality. Thus, Harm Sorley sifts through the tatters of a memory ruined by alcohol and prison life, struggling to understand his present predicament as he makes his way home through the mountains. As he tries to make sense of his fragmented world he is a sort of twentieth-century everyman, searching for clues through the labyrinth of a world that no longer makes sense. Harm, like many of the characters in McCrumb's world, is searching for Thomas Wolfe's "lost lane-end into heaven" but finds himself, in Wolfe's words (echoed by Nora Bonesteel in the novel): "forever prison-pent" and "forever a stranger and alone."[6]

Harm's former wife, Rita, makes her own journey of remembrance, triggered by hearing of his prison-break. Forsaking her beige and pastel world of middle-class respectability, Rita returns to an old shell of a blue trailer on a patch of barren land, believing, as she tells her daughter Charlotte, "sometimes you just have to look at the past to figure out where you're going."[7] In numerous ways, *She Walks These Hills* echoes Rita's hard-won wisdom as many characters examine the past—personal and historical—in order to find a meaningful sense of reality. The stories of Harm and Katie draw two relative outsiders, Henry Kretzer, a radio personality who calls himself "Hank the Yank" and Jeremy Cobb, a doctoral student in ethno-history at Virginia Tech, to attempt to reconstruct the past. Both characters begin with simplistic pictures. For Hank, Harm Sorley is first a joke, then a folk-hero, and finally, a man who deserves a fair shake. For Jeremy, Katie Wyler is at first a fascinating and romantic piece of history, an "image in stained glass," pretty and dynamic.[8] As Hank and Jeremy move closer to the literal mountain homes of the figures they are researching they discover a reality more complex and human than the myths they began with.

---

[6] McCrumb, *Hills,* 420.
[7] McCrumb, *Hills*, 196.
[8] McCrumb, *Hills*, 77

As the story progresses, Harm and Katie serve as catalysts for discovery in the lives of a number of characters. Some simply come to a clearer understanding of the facts and to sympathy with the plights of the fugitives. But, in McCrumb's magical world, some come face to face with a living past or painful present to which they are bound by sympathy and suffering. At the Sorley farm, Chalarty comes face to face with her real father and her love for him, acknowledging herself a child of the hills. In the wilderness, Nora Bonesteel, gifted with "the Sight;"[9] Jeremy Cobb, struggling to survive; and Harm Sorley, a fellow fugitive, all come face to face with Katie Wyler in a "wilderness devoid of all temporal landmarks" forever "swallowing the years in its green silence."[10]

The idea of connections between the ever-changing world of time and the changeless world of eternity is itself ancient. The Celtic ancestors of McCrumb's mountain folk believed that there were times, places, circumstances, and souls where the wall between the worlds was thin and communication between them possible. In McCrumb's novel, this ancient belief becomes a means of exploring and questioning the ways modernization has uprooted families and individuals and threatened even the land itself. Unlike these popular writers who celebrate folkways and nature with idealizing nostalgia, McCrumb clearly realizes that remembering the past while adjusting to the future is a difficult and complex task. Any character in her novel who starts out constructing a "romance" of the past as Hank and Jeremy do, soon finds that the past is tougher and more solid than any dream.

One of the ways McCrumb shatters the romance of past is through events and characters in which history seems to be repeating itself. Central among these is the story of Sabrina Harkryder, the sullen and slovenly teenaged mother who murders her baby in the present of the story. As Jeremy Cobb stumbles through the last leg of his wilderness journey in the company of both the ghostly Katie and the all too real Sabrina, he sees them as a study in opposites. Yet, he learns from Nora Bonesteel that his heroic pioneer fugitive and this ignorant and desperate

---

[9] McCrumb, *Hills*, 12.
[10] McCrumb, *Hills*, 340.

twentieth-century teenager share the closest bond of all. Both women did what they felt they had to in order to escape an intolerable situation, and for each, the price of freedom was the death of her baby.

At one point, Sabrina, trashy and ignorant, utters one of the novel's central statements about the complexity of human life. Responding to Jeremy's romantic picture of Katie Wyler making her long journey out of love for Rab Greer, Sabrina says, "Choices aren't that simple, mister." And, she adds, "I think people can get caught between a rock and a hard place, and then there's no right answers without somebody getting hurt."[11] Her words underscore a repeated motif of the novel, embodied in the murders of Claib Maggard, Dustin Allison Harkryder, and Katie's nameless child, and in the suicides of Harm Sorley and Patrick Allan Kendrick.

Along with the complexities of moral choice, the novel also ponders the complexities of change, weighing the conveniences and opportunities of modern life against the customs and connections of an earlier time. For many of the characters, change is associated with a diminishing world, "each year more stale and colorless than the one before."[12] The novel echoes with laments for the passing of chestnut trees, wolves, mountain panthers, timber rattlers, and "hillbillies" whose families have lived on the land and loved it for over two hundred years. The diminishing world is embodied in characters like Euell Pentland, who scorns mountain crafts and music, preferring the homogenized world of Lawrence Welk.[13] It is also revealed in various characters' statements about how "times have changed" and usually not for the better, as Sheriff Arrowood suggests when he laments that the law has grown more civilized while the outlaws have grown more deadly.[14]

Yet the face of change looks different to different characters and not all of them cope with change in the same way. Trapped in one particular time, Harm Sorley can only see the modern houses dotting the mountains as "ugly"[15] and "glass cages."[16] Thoroughly rooted in the past and

---

[11] McCrumb, *Hills*, 394.

[12] McCrumb, *Hills*, 31.

[13] McCrumb, *Hills,* 196.

[14] McCrumb, *Hills,* 196

[15] McCrumb, *Hills*, 179.

reluctantly seeing into the future, Nora Bonesteel seems to have reached a civilized compromise with change. She practices the old folkways, such as telling the bees that Geneva Albright has died. But she has also changed the face of her "ancient farmhouse," putting in new floor-to-ceiling windows that embrace the mountain vista.[17] After his trek through the wilderness in which he discards the "burden of civilization"[18] then longs to finds his way back to it, Jeremy Cobb sees Nora's house as "like civilization as he wanted it to be, and as he had never found it."[19]

Though characters in *She Walks These Hills* always pay a price for change, sometimes that change is good. This seems particularly true of changes for Appalachian women through education and opportunities to work. While Sabrina Harkryder and Crystal Stanley remain trapped in a world of dependency and sexual barter, Charlotte Pentland and Martha Ayers represent new possibilities for women. Charlotte sees her education as a means of independence, declaring, "At least *I* won't be poor or dependent on some man all my life."[20] One of the central subplots of the novel concerns Martha Ayers' campaign to prove herself worthy of a promotion from dispatcher to deputy and a place in what had traditionally been a man's world. When Spencer Arrowood protests that the deputy's job is dangerous, Martha replies, "Hell, Spencer. Women get beat up by enraged husbands, gang-raped by good ol' boys, and hunted like deer by serial killers. Being a woman is dangerous. I'm just asking you to give me a gun and more money to make up for it."[21]

As the novel progresses, the deaths of Katie Wyler and Rita Pentland vividly illustrate Martha's point about the vulnerability of women in the traditional world of female dependency. Yet, as Martha struggles to better herself by launching a one-woman manhunt to find Harm, Joe LeDonne, Martha's lover, has trouble coping with the shift from Martha as respectful listener to Martha as participant. He responds by withdrawing and by sleeping with the desperately available Crystal

---

[16] McCrumb, *Hills,* 203.

[17] McCrumb, *Hills,* 168.

[18] McCrumb, *Hills,* 163–64.

[19] McCrumb, *Hills,* 419.

[20] McCrumb, *Hills,* 300.

[21] McCrumb, *Hills,* 77.

Stanley. In the end, however, Joe manages to accept the change, coming to respect Martha's work and reconciling himself to the growing equality in their relationship.

Most changes in the novel, however, seem to create more problems than they solve as the forces of modernization threaten the extinction of a way of life and of the savage and beloved wilderness. Throughout the narrative, the words of Nora Bonesteel and Hank the Yank operate as a chorus, commenting on the action and reminding the reader of the larger implications of the character's stories as they unfold. Both Nora and Hank see Harm Sorley in the context of a struggle between those who belong to the land and love it and those who come to the land as tourists and consumers, intent on what they can wring out of it. Sometimes the exploitation of relative outsiders is trivial: Hank the Yank's "Harm Sorley" bumper stickers and t-shirts, Buck Pentland's using the glamour of his hillbilly connections to seduce coeds. But its murderous possibilities are dramatized in the ostensibly respectable characters of Claib Maggard, who steals from his neighbors and deliberately poisons Harm Sorley's land, and of Euell Pentland, who murders his wife. These men represent an attitude toward nature and toward people that may ultimately result in large-scale destruction.

Nora and Hank lament the passing of wolves and other wildlife, the dispossession of the Native Americans, and now, the dispossession of the "hillbillies" who have lived on the land for two hundred years. But theirs is not just a poetic refrain in a world where Hank finds syrupy chemicals oozing out of the barren ground of Harm's deserted farm and Harm himself notes the trees dying on the highest ridges, the victims of another sort of pollution.[22] Newcomers and bureaucratic bullies like Claib and Euell see the land and its people as something to be used—even used up, for pleasure and profit. Their world makes a mountain man like Harm Sorley a "throwaway," who escapes the prison of their injustice by managing to get himself literally hauled away with the garbage.[23] To the owner of one of those glass cages on the mountain, Harm is simply part of the local "fauna," "riffraff" like the deer and raccoons, a nuisance to

---

[22] McCrumb, *Hills*, 279.
[23] McCrumb, *Hills*, 42.

be disposed of.[24] When people like this fail to see the wilderness and its creatures as a context of survival, they may, McCrumb hints, be preparing for their own doom. Toward the end of the novel, Hank the Yank cites the naturalist David Brower, "The wild places are where we began. When they end, so do we."[25]

The novel is threaded with such quotations from literary writers, old hymns, and popular songs that underscore the concerns voiced by Nora, Hank and other characters who seek a reality grounded in justice and love in the midst of an exploitative world. Yet McCrumb is aware of the violence and injustice of the mountain culture as well as of the modern world. The traditional "guns and honor" culture of the southeast is as much a part of the tragedies of the novel as is the greed and indifference of an industrial, consumer society.[26] McCrumb's characters live in a beautiful but dangerous world in which, in the last analysis, most folks must simply, like Sabrina Harkryder, "do what you have to do."[27] Yet there is hope. In a society that throws away poor men like Harm Sorley for defending his way of life, there are crusaders like Hank the Yank protesting against the travesties of justice symbolized by "hanging the elephant."[28] While Rab Greer murders Katie Wyler, Martha Ayers reigns in her murderous fantasies and contents herself with warning off Crystal Stanley.

In the character of Jeremy Cobb, McCrumb reminds us that any flight from twentieth-century realities can only be temporary. While his romantic vision of Katie Wyler is replaced by a ragged, dirty, emaciated reality, that reality enables Jeremy to glimpse the struggle to survive at the heart of all existence. Late in the novel Sheriff Arrowood says, "love is just as strong as those things primordial."[29] Though Jeremy fears that love has somehow diminished in the modern era, Rita's return to Harm and Joe's return to Martha suggest that love is the thread through the

---

[24] McCrumb, *Hills,* 202.
[25] McCrumb, *Hills,* 434.
[26] McCrumb, *Hills, 239.*
[27] McCrumb, *Hills,* 412.
[28] McCrumb, *Hills,* 264, 313.
[29] McCrumb, *Hills,* 434.

serpentine chain.[30] In *She Walks These Hills* love—between parents and children, women and men, people and the land—may be faltering, imperfect, and even dangerous. Yet it can triumph over hatred and shame, calling Rita and Charlotte Pentland back to Harm and keeping LeDonne and Martha together.

Love is one of the central values of the mountain home that is both a place of captivity—the "prisoning hills" of the novel's epigraph from James Still's "Heritage"—and of belonging. It is the backbone of the families that are also both imprisoning and a cardinal ground of identity. But love in *She Walks These Hills* is a tough love, seasoned and largely unsentimental. Its nature is perhaps most clearly stated in the words Nora Bonesteel borrows from Mother Jones, "Pray for the dead and fight like hell for the living."[31] It makes a poor and ignorant man like Harm Sorley a better parent than Euell Pentland or Jeremy Cobb's middle class mom and dad can hope to be.[32] It calls even strangers to honor dead wanderers like Katie and Harm and to fight—not always successfully—for the survival of escaped convicts, white trash babies, Eagle Scouts, and housewives in beige polyester pantsuits.

Perhaps it is a form of this love that enables McCrumb and many of her strongest characters to fight for the last vestiges of a world that is passing away. We may not, she realizes, be able to save it. But we can at least recognize and respect and remember it. We can cheer on Charlotte Pentland when she reaches out to embrace a heritage that has left its traces on her speech, despite her academic training. We can join Hank the Yank's "electronic wake" for Harm Sorley, recognizing that Stephen Benet's "moonshiner" and "lost, wild-rabbit of a girl" were part of a world in many ways richer, though a thousand times more rugged, than our own.[33] Like chestnut trees and wolves and people we have loved, they are irreplaceable. When they are gone, "Something will pass that was American/And all the movies will not bring it back."[34] While no novel can bring it back either, *She Walks These Hills*, like the oral history

---

[30] McCrumb, *Hills,* 343.
[31] McCrumb, *Hills,* 14.
[32] McCrumb, *Hills,* 233.
[33] McCrumb, *Hills,* 444.
[34] McCrumb, Hills, 444.

and culture it celebrates, is a link in a chain of serpentine that stretches back to a time before the Celtic tribes were scattered, back to the time when the mountains were severed. It exists to remind us not only of what we have lost, but also of what survives and what may be saved, and of the enduring power of love and memory.

"Based on a True-Story"

Using *The Ballad of Frankie Silver* to Teach the Conventions of Narrative

Lana Whited

Most students probably think of fictional and nonfictional literature as water drawn from two very different wells: fiction from the writer's imagination and nonfiction from the "real" life of the writer or someone else. This distinction between fiction and nonfiction focuses on the aspect of literature we usually emphasize when teaching it to students: content. However, it is equally important for students to understand the *mechanics* of literature, including how a writer crafts his or her material and how the text establishes expectations in a reader. Examining a narrative drawn from fact, such as Sharyn McCrumb's 1998 novel *The Ballad of Frankie Silver*, can deepen students' understanding of what writers do, how writing works, and why literature matters.

McCrumb's book operates in two layers. The outer layer is the story of Spencer Arrowood, sheriff of Wake County, Tennessee, who has been invited to the execution of Fate Harkryder. Arrowood's investigation and testimony helped send Harkryder to death row, but with the execution invitation in hand, the sheriff begins to question Harkryder's guilt. His musings remind him of a story told to him by his predecessor Nelse Miller in a North Carolina hillside cemetery—the story of Frankie Silver, who was hanged for murder in Morganton, North Carolina, on 12 July 1833. Miller told Arrowood, "There's only two murder cases in these mountains that I'm not happy with....One is the fellow you're about to put on death row. And the other one is Frankie Silver."[1]

The Arrowood story is the product of McCrumb's imagination, and the Stewart-Silver story is the result of her painstaking research. By weaving together the two, McCrumb has created a unique work, which bridges the fact/fiction gap. Thus, a reader of *The Ballad of Frankie Silver* can explore differences in the purpose, technique, and reader response of fictional and nonfictional material in *one* book.

On 10 January 1832, eighteen-year-old Frances Stewart Silver, her mother Barbara and brother Blackston were taken to jail in Morganton, accused of the murder of Frankie's husband Charlie, whom Frankie reported missing on 23 December 1831. Barbara and Blackston Stewart were released seven days after their arrest, due to lack of evidence, but in March 1832, Frankie was indicted by a Burke County grand jury, convicted, and sentenced to be hanged in July. An unsuccessful appeal to the North Carolina Supreme Court and a change of local judges delayed the execution, and she was finally hanged on 12 July 1833.

Interest in the Frankie Silver story was revived in the late 1990s, when the only two book-length works devoted to the material were published, both in 1998. The same year, Appalachian filmmaker Tom Davenport released a documentary on the case, produced in conjunction with the University of North Carolina Folklore Curriculum. In addition to *The Ballad of Frankie Silver*, the fifth book in Sharyn McCrumb's "ballad novel" series, the year brought *The Untold Story of Frankie Silver* by Chapel Hill, North Carolina, journalist Perry Deane Young. Interestingly, both McCrumb and Young have ties to the case: McCrumb is a distant cousin of Frankie Silver (on the Stewart side), and Young is a native of Burke County whose ancestors there pre-date Frankie Silver's trial and execution.

---

[1] Sharyn McCrumb, *The Ballad of Frankie Silver* (New York: Dutton, 1998) 15.

An important distinction must be made between McCrumb's and Young's work. While their research involved many of the same documents and interviews, as well as footwork along the same paths, their results are very different. McCrumb's book, as its cover attests, is a novel. While McCrumb's research into the Frankie Silver case formed the basis for her inner story, the plot involving the impending execution of Lafayette "Fate" Harkryder in the late twentieth century is fictional. McCrumb's overall purpose in using two narrative layers is to contrast "poor people as defendants and rich people as officers of the court,...Celt versus English values in developing America, ...mountain people versus the 'flatlanders' in any culture."[2] Through this contrast, McCrumb hopes to underscore the common theme of Frankie Silver's and Fate Harkryder's stories: that, in the words of the book's epigram (from Truman Capote's *In Cold Blood*), "The rich never hang; only the poor and friendless." Theme, then, is the overriding concern of *The Ballad of Frankie Silver*.

Young's book, by contrast, is primarily devoted to accuracy and establishing "The Untold Story" of the case. Young aims to correct over 150 years of fabulous legend engendered by Frankie Silver's story. The structure of his book reinforces this purpose, as he begins by spinning out a yarn about the young woman, which he claims is much like the tales told before Western North Carolina mountain hearths since the notorious crime. Then, in the book's longest section, "The Search for Facts about Frankie and Charlie Silver," he provides a virtual reference book about the case. The chapter headings in this section reinforce his aim: "The Silvers," "The Stewarts," "Morganton Then," "The Members of the Court," "The Escape," and so forth. After thoroughly reviewing the case, Young deals with the ballad itself—the song Frankie Silver was erroneously reported to have sung from the gallows. Section IV of Young's book consists of original documents related to the case, such as newspaper accounts, court documents, and letters and petitions soliciting Frankie's clemency. The book ends with a three-page bibliography. Ultimately, Young's book examines the tension between fact and

---

[2] McCrumb, *Ballad*, 384.

folklore. It would be a useful reference for a student reading McCrumb's novel.

Having students compare McCrumb's and Young's purposes would be a worthwhile exercise highlighting the aims of fiction. For that reason, the optimum experience for students would be reading both books. If this is impossible, literature students who had read *The Ballad of Frankie Silver* could examine some contrasting elements between it and *The Untold Story of Frankie Silver* simply by examining Young's table of contents, which could be easily photocopied. (By contrast, students in a social studies class who had read Young's book could examine how individual episodes are dramatized in McCrumb's novel). A teacher could start a meaningful discussion by asking students to consider why Young's book includes such a table while McCrumb's does not, and how the answer to that question reflects the writers' differing purposes.

Whether or not students also read Young's book, a teacher could also ask them to contrast the two titles and explain what they expect from each book. Even students inexperienced in literary criticism should see that Young's title, *The Untold Story*...promises to deliver truths as yet unrevealed, while McCrumb's *The Ballad of*...leads readers to expect something more literary or artistic, a rendering of the facts, rather than just the facts themselves. This question should be asked *before* students have read either book, to get a true impression of the expectations raised by the titles. When I teach *In Cold Blood*, I always ask students to stop on the third page and explain what they think Truman Capote means when he describes "four shotgun blasts that, all told, ended six human lives."[3] After the usual jokes about bullets passing through people and into others, some students in the class can always guess that Capote may be referring to murders followed by legal executions. If nothing else, they are intrigued to read on in order to learn how the "four into six" equation works out. Research into reading comprehension suggests that students who get the most out of a text consciously or intuitively apply pre-reading strategies. Major prescribed systems for reading, such as "PQ3R" or "SQ3R," always begin with the stage of previewing or surveying a text. Asking students to discuss the title and front material

---

[3] Truman Capote, *In Cold Blood* (New York: Random House, 1965) 15.

before delving into the story would reinforce the importance of the often-overlooked stages of previewing and questioning.[4]

Also, before reading very far into the story, students should be asked whether knowing that a story is based on fact changes their feelings about reading it. Do they take the story any more seriously than one they don't know to be true, for example? Students have enough experience with movies based on factual events to be able to draw some parallels in answering this question. Alternately, the *Blair Witch Project* phenomenon during the summer of 1999 can provide a useful corollary, as many viewers of that film regarded and discussed it as though it were a true story (a misperception which the film's official website encouraged).[5]

Teachers should ask such questions before students begin their reading and again when they have completed the book, to provide students an opportunity to talk about whether and how their perceptions have changed. After completing the book, students should be prepared for more difficult questions: In encouraging viewers of the *Blair Witch Project* to view the film as fact-based, are the promoters suggesting that the film would be more valuable if the story were true? If so, does the same principle apply to a novel? In other words, would *The Ballad of Frankie Silver* be less valuable or "good" if it were all a product of Sharyn McCrumb's imagination? Is the Frankie Silver story of greater worth than the Fate Harkryder plot because hers is true and his is not? Do we view or judge a work differently after learning that it is not true? Is there a kind of truth which is different from factuality? (Here I have in mind the concept of verisimilitude.) A teacher's ultimate goal in such a

---

[4] The stages in PQ3R and SQ3R vary slightly, depending on study skills texts. The sequence of letters generally represents Preview (or Survey), Question, Read, Recite, and Review.

[5] Besides the *Blair Witch Project*, which a majority of young people have probably seen, many other films are based on a blending of fact and fiction. *Titanic* and *Amistad* are prominent examples. In addition, it is interesting that filmmakers Joel and Ethan Coen provide a note in the opening credits of their film *Fargo* that it is "based on a true story," even though the routine "Any resemblance to any persons living or dead..." disclaimer appears at the end. Students might be asked, regarding the *Blair Witch Project* and *Fargo*, why filmmakers would want to give a film the appearance of being factual when it is not.

discussion is to get students to make some generalizations about how their expectations for fiction and nonfiction are different.

An important aspect of reading *The Ballad of Frankie Silver* for a student should be scrutinizing how McCrumb weaves primary written sources into her text. These fall primarily into two categories: court documents and letters. Three court documents are reproduced in the text, including the following: an arrest warrant naming "Frankey [sic] Silver and Barbara and Blackston Stewart",[6] (signed 9 January 1832); a writ of habeas corpus issued after Frankie's father, Isaiah Stewart, complained that his daughter, wife, and son had not been formally charged (dated 13 January 1832),[7] and the denial of Frankie's appeal to the North Carolina Supreme Court, a three-sentence document which arrived in Morganton in July 1832.[8]

In addition, McCrumb reproduces the text of four original letters. The first is from David Newland, owner of the stagecoach line, which carried people and news back and forth from Morganton to Raleigh. Newland's letter, written on 6 September 1832, to Governor Montfort Stokes, was accompanied by a petition containing 113 names (including those of four jurors) and declaring Frankie Silver "a fit subject for excitive [sic] Clemency."[9] The second letter is from Silver's attorney Thomas Wilson to the governor, dated 19 November 1832, informing him that Frankie had gotten the impression from Newland's petition that she would be pardoned and asking if the governor had reached a decision.[10] A letter dated 29 June 1833, from Mary E. Erwin to Governor David L. Swain (who succeeded Stokes), encouraged Swain to pardon Frankie on the grounds that Charlie Silver's "treatment of her was both unbecoming and cruel verry [sic] often" and that the condemned woman had a young child.[11] McCrumb writes, "Appended to this carefully

---

[6] McCrumb, *Ballad*, 27. McCrumb standardizes the language of the original warrant. For example, she changes the spelling to Stewart from Stuard, as it appears on the original warrant, and standardizes the spelling of Elijah Green's name.

[7] McCrumb, *Ballad*, 72.

[8] McCrumb, *Ballad,* 222.

[9] McCrumb, *Ballad,* 226.

[10] McCrumb, *Ballad,* 235–36.

[11] McCrumb, *Ballad*, 276–77.

wrought document were the signatures of nearly every gentlewoman in [Burke] county."[12] The fourth letter is a reply of three (albeit long) sentences from Governor Swain, who claims his reply will arrive too late to save Frankie Silver and that all he can do is hope "that she may find that mercy in Heaven which seemed to be necessarily denied upon earth."[13] Swain's reply, dated 9 July 1833, was apparently timed to arrive in Morganton on the eve of the execution, too late for anyone to inform him that there was still time for a pardon.

Students reading *The Ballad of Frankie Silver* should be encouraged to examine how McCrumb works each original document into the text. For example, after she reproduces Governor Swain's letter, the author concludes that chapter with dialogue between Clerk Gaither and W.C. Bevins, author of a letter accompanying a recent petition (late June 1833). The point of this imagined conversation is Gaither's and Bevins' confusion over how Swain could have thought he lacked the time to pardon Frankie Silver. McCrumb's purpose is clearly to expose Swain's underhanded tactics. The chapter concludes with Gaither's question, "why equivocate with this pretended misunderstanding of dates? Why did he not simply say, *I refuse to pardon the prisoner*"[?] and Bevins' reply, "He has said it, Mr. Gaither. As plainly as any politician ever spoke."[14] Examination of the context McCrumb sets around these original documents can help students understand how a writer can use factual material for rhetorical aims.

In a number of instances, McCrumb refers to or draws upon original materials that she does not reproduce verbatim. An interesting discussion might involve why she chooses to include some explicitly and make overt reference to others. For example, before the prisoner leaves the jail for the gallows, Burgess Gaither informs her that he is required to re-read the judge's order for her death. However, the text of this document is not repeated at this point, probably because it is Gaither's reaction that McCrumb wants to highlight. "I found that the paper was shaking as I began to read from it," the clerk says, "and it was then that I realized I

---

[12] McCrumb, *Ballad,* 277.
[13] McCrumb, *Ballad*, 284.
[14] McCrumb, *Ballad*, 285.

was as unstrung as the rest of them."[15] If an officer of the court is "unstrung" by the impending execution, surely that execution is questionable. Again, McCrumb arranges her material for the desired effect, which the reading of a document in eighteenth-century legalese might destroy.

Another interesting omission is McCrumb's decision to paraphrase events concerning the bill of indictment against Frankie. Clearly, the reading of the charges, a document of 383 words all in *one* sentence, marked a pivotal stage of the legal proceedings. On its reverse side were the words, "A true bill as to Francis Silver. Not True Bill as to the others."[16] Thus, it dismisses the charges against Frankie's family members—a development whose relevance grows as a reader learns more about the crime. Despite its significance, McCrumb does not reproduce it. Instead, she focuses on the political context of the charges—Sheriff Sam Tate's concern that none of the suspects will be convicted if all are charged. Thus, McCrumb paraphrases the brief statement on the back of the indictment to Tate's decision, "Here's what I propose that we do, boys: we bring back a true bill on Mrs. Frances Silver, and we no-bill her mother and brother. We know she's in it up to her neck, and I'd rather see her punished for her crime than cast the net too wide and risk losing all three."[17] Again, McCrumb focuses attention on the political backdrop of the case, reinforcing the focus on Frankie as scapegoat for a guilty family.

It is also important for students to understand that historical facts can be unclear and that two different writers can make conflicting decisions about representing history. For example, a major controversy in the Frankie Silver material is the question of who defended the young woman, as her attorney is not named in court documents. Perry Young says that Thomas Wilson was Frankie Silver's sole solicitor, and the notion that she was represented by Woodfin is "one of the more common errors in the stories that have been published."[18] However, Sharyn

---

[15] McCrumb, *Ballad,* 311.

[16] Perry Deane Young, *The Untold Story of Frankie Silver* (Asheboro NC: Down Home, 1998) 134.

[17] McCrumb, *Ballad,* 126–27.

[18] Young, *Untold,* 18.

McCrumb has Frankie defended by the well-known and flamboyant Asheville attorney Nicholas Woodfin, with Morganton resident Thomas Wilson as co-counsel. McCrumb explains in her afterword that a North Carolina district attorney's explanation of 1830s criminal law convinced her of the accuracy of her account.[19] Having students examine these conflicting accounts and review the basis for each could be a valuable lesson in the use of sources. Students should also discuss the fact that some disagreements about historical fact may be unresolved or unresolvable, particularly in a case such as Frankie Silver's, as her attorney is not named in primary documents.

Finally, from the use of original materials and the dual-time perspective in *The Ballad of Frankie Silver*, students can learn something about the style or texture of narrative. In the present-day plot, characters talk like we do today, with the occasional east Tennessee mountains flavor of lines such as, "Afternoon, Miz Bonesteel! I've come to sit a spell"[20] and "I reckon it's too late to put the lights out and pretend we're not here."[21] In the 1830s plot, however, McCrumb faces the challenge of recreating the speech of both an educated, upper-middle-class man and an unschooled mountain girl. She must write, for Burgess Gaither, lines such as "When my expression did not change, the constable must have realized that such rustic deductions were wasted upon gentlemen, for we lacked the requisite frontier skills to recognize the significance of that discovery."[22] And just a few pages later, she must have Frankie thinking, "I see you looking at me, Constable Charlie Baker. I know you of old. Your daddy fought in the Revolution, and your brother is the justice of the peace, so you have land and position, but for all that you are a runty fellow with never a smile for ary soul."[23] Comparing the language of characters of differing dialects and speech habits can help students to understand the concept of voice in writing, how a writer achieves a

[19] McCrumb, *Ballad,* 382 83.
[20] McCrumb, *Ballad,* 20.
[21] McCrumb, *Ballad,* 48.
[22] McCrumb, *Ballad,* 39.
[23] McCrumb, *Ballad,* 41.

character's voice, and how (and why) one character's voice is different from another's. [24]

It is also valuable for students to know that dialect in fiction is often frowned upon by New York editors and literary agents. While McCrumb uses some aspects of dialect in *The Ballad of Frankie Silver*, such as Frankie's use of the word "ary" for "any," the writing is not heavily dialectal, even in the speech of the characters most likely to use dialect. Students should also be asked to talk about how much the speech of characters like Frankie may be standardized or even romanticized. Where, for example, does a reader find Frankie using an expression she wouldn't likely use or a word she wouldn't likely know? William Faulkner said of his novel *The Sound and the Fury* that he gave the mentally retarded boy-man Benjy Compson the language he would have used, if he could articulate his own experience. Similarly, students should consider where Sharyn McCrumb might lend language to Frankie Silver, so that the mountain girl/woman can express her experience more vividly, or with literary effect. A related and equally important point is how a fiction writer avoids stereotyping or patronizing a character through the representation of language.

Students can learn a lot about how narrative is shaped and the decisions a writer makes in shaping it from examination of the original materials and how McCrumb works them into the novel. The materials not reproduced in the book are readily available, without a trip to the Morganton courthouse or the North Carolina archives. Young reproduces all the relevant documents in Part IV of his book, and a website created and maintained by Frankie Silver's great-great-great granddaughter in Georgia includes facsimiles and transcriptions of the Complaint and Arrest Warrant, the Bill of Indictment, and the Writ of Habeas Corpus. Thus, the documents could be easily printed and reproduced for student examination—or students could be encouraged to put their Internet skills to use and retrieve the documents themselves. The web site *Frankie*

---

[24] For students unfamiliar with the dialects of the western North Carolina mountains, teachers could show Tom Davenport's film the *Ballad of Frankie Silver*, a documentary featuring western North Carolina native Bobby McMillon, a musician and storyteller. McMillon's speech is characterized by many aspects of a dialect similar in its origins to Frankie Silver's.

Stewart Silver's Memorial Page includes gravesite photos and other interesting information about the case (www.frankiesilver.com). A good starting point for Internet research on the case is *Frankie Silver Resources* (www.ferrum.edu/lwhited/silver.htm).[25]

By examining similarities between the fictional and nonfictional accounts of the case, students can also be encouraged to see some basic priniciples of all narrative. For example, a fictional story such as McCrumb's Fate Harkryder plot in *The Ballad of Frankie Silver,* which springs primarily from the writer's imagination may still involve substantial research. McCrumb, in her afterword, acknowledges the assistance of an attorney, a law enforcement officer, and a death row inmate in helping her establish the complexity of a capital case, particularly an execution. McCrumb also visited Riverbend, a maximum-security prison in Nashville which houses Tennessee's death row.[26] A teacher should point out these acknowledgements in the afterword to call students' attention to McCrumb's attempt to achieve verisimilitude. Students can also be encouraged to pick out selections in the text which are probably based on research, such as McCrumb's explanation of the origin of Tennessee's electric chair toward the end of chapter 1.[27] This exercise in the origin of information can help novice readers understand how narrative is made. Students should also note that McCrumb included the afterword and bibliography, whose presence can lead to a discussion about acknowledgement of sources, even in a fictional work.

In addition, students should be asked why McCrumb didn't place her acknowledgements at the beginning of the book. Such placement might have given away important plot details, and this answer can open the door to a discussion of suspense, an important aspect of all narrative. Whether a novel is based primarily on historical material or the writer's imagination, the shape of the narrative will be largely the same, beginning with an exposition which features a complication, then rising in action to a point of climax, followed by a denouement. Throughout

---

[25] This web site was created by the author in May 2000 with funding from the Appalachian College Association. It may be accessed directly via the URL or from the ACA's web site at www.acaweb.org.

[26] McCrumb, *Ballad,* 383–84.

[27] McCrumb, *Ballad,* 21–23.

this process, a writer wants to keep a reader guessing. Students should be encouraged to apply the basic plot outline to both McCrumb's outer and inner plots, and then to go a step further: to actually diagram the two plots in a parallel fashion, on the same page or two separate pages laid side by side. This step will allow students to see how major developments in one plot correspond to those in the other. (This diagramming is particularly useful to visual learners.)

The best example of this parallel plot technique occurs late in the novel, when Sheriff Spencer Arrowood visits the location of the Silvers' cabin with Nora Bonesteel, relying on Nora's gift of "the sight" to help him understand the murder of Charlie Silver. Arrowood realizes that Frankie must have had help from her family in dismembering Charlie and cleaning up the crime scene and that it was probably this help her father urged her to keep secret in his admonition "Die with it in you!" as she stood on the gallows. The sheriff is then able to figure out that Fate Harkryder is also taking the blame, because he was a minor, for a crime his brothers almost certainly committed. At this point in the narrative, Arrowood has already assembled all the facts he needs to understand both cases, but it is not until he stands near the Silver cabin's hearthstone that he is able to put in the final pieces and see the whole puzzle—or, more appropriately, both puzzles. By the end of the chapter, Arrowood articulates the connection between the two cases that a reader has already glimpsed. Arrowood says, "I think I understand what bothered Nelse Miller about the case now. I know why Frankie Silver has been on my mind."[28] At this point, he actively begins trying to save Fate Harkryder. In the very next chapter, Fate Harkryder is presented with an opportunity to avoid dying with his knowledge in him, and his refusal to implicate his brothers suggests that the golden rule in mountain families of protecting one's blood kin has not changed in 155 years. McCrumb's novel is ultimately the story of two young people sacrificed on the altar of this mountain code.

But in encouraging students to see parallels between the two plots, a teacher wouldn't want to start near the end of the novel. They are plenty of earlier examples. Nora Bonesteel is introduced in chapter 1, when

---

[28] McCrumb, *Ballad*, 352.

Pauline Harkryder visits her to confirm her own intuition that her nephew Fate is innocent and to learn whether intervention might be fruitful. In a masterful association, McCrumb moves a reader along from the power of Bonesteel's "sight" to the current of the Tennessee electric chair, a power that threatens to transform Fate. The chapter ends with a few examples of prison folklore about "Old Sparky," such as how the chair is tested once a month. This brief disquisition on modern-day execution ends with the word "legend," and the reader turns the page to confront the sentence, "I remember the first time I ever heard of Frankie Silver."[29] Thus, McCrumb establishes the connection between the question of Fate Harkryder's innocence and the Silver case.

After the chapter detailing Frankie's arrest, McCrumb cuts back to a chapter in which Spencer Arrowood recalls the crimes for which Fate Harkryder was convicted.[30] At this point in the narrative, Arrowood's deputy Martha Ayers intrudes, bringing a Mrs. Honeycutt whom she has conveniently met at the public library while looking for the Frankie Silver materials Arrowood has requested. On the heels of the sheriff's recollection of the earlier crime, Mrs. Honeycutt (a native of western North Carolina) spins out the tale of Frankie and Charlie Silver.[31] Chapter 3 concludes with Fate Harkryder pondering all the lawyers he's had during his legal proceedings, and in the next 1830s chapter, when McCrumb cuts back to Burgess Gaither, the case against Frankie Silver has proceeded to the point of "Choosing Counsel."[32] Such parallels continue throughout the novel, and mapping them would help students understand how McCrumb juxtaposes the details of her two plots.

Contrasting the two narrative levels of *The Ballad of Frankie Silver* can also be an education in point of view. Frankie Silver's story is narrated in first person by Burgess Gaither, the young Burke County clerk of court. Students should be prodded to see that Gaither is an appropriate narrator because he is socioeconomically somewhere between the upstanding, affluent Erwins of Morganton and the "hillbilly"

---

[29] McCrumb, *Ballad,* 24.
[30] McCrumb, *Ballad,* 47–48.
[31] McCrumb, *Ballad,* 50–54.
[32] McCrumb, *Ballad,* 104.

Stewarts. Gaither describes himself as "an outsider in the ranks of the aristocracy."[33] Also, as court clerk, he is always present at the crucial milestones in Frankie's case and thus can report them with first-hand knowledge. It would also be useful to have students briefly discuss why other characters in the 1830s plot would be inferior to Gaither as narrators. The attorneys, for example, are too biased to be trustworthy narrators, and none of the female characters would have had sufficient access to events at that time to know what Gaither knows. It is also noteworthy that Gaither was very close to Frankie Silver's age at the time of her trial, making him a suitable contemporary. Finally, only a character with the benefit of Gaither's education and social standing could portray both sides of the socioeconomic gulf, which is McCrumb's main theme.

The Spencer Arrowood/Fate Harkryder plot is told by a third-person omniscient narrator, usually (but not exclusively) limited to Arrowood's point of view. During the sheriff's attempt to piece together the stories of Frankie Silver and Fate Harkryder, a reader inhabits his consciousness, and it would be worthwhile to have students talk about what this perspective contributes. In this discussion, it is important to ask students to consider Arrowood as a stand-in for a reader also trying to sort out the details of both cases. They should also be encouraged to see the sheriff as a surrogate for the novelist herself. McCrumb told an interviewer in 1997, "I've always been somebody who was looking for patterns. I have...a comparative sort of mind.... The searching for patterns is always the first step toward telling stories" (McCrumb, Interview). It seems especially true that the novelist drawing on historical materials should be looking for patterns—in McCrumb's case, patterns of justice—or injustice—in two mountain murder cases 150 years apart, one real, one fictional.

A further study in point of view could be undertaken by asking students to examine the brief interludes when readers are given Frankie's and Fate's perspectives. In several 1830s chapters, a reader is treated to Frankie's first-person reactions to the events around her. These passages are italicized in the text and placed at the ends of chapters. Interestingly,

[33] McCrumb, *Ballad,* 319.

McCrumb withholds Frankie's point of view during four entire sections covering her trial, conviction, sentencing, and appeal. A reader does not hear from Frankie directly from page 139, when her lawyer is selected, until her notorious escape, narrated in a section which begins on page 252. Students should be encouraged to think about the reasons for the silence and to see its consistency with the historical fact that Frankie did not testify on her own behalf.

Harkryder's thoughts, also generally placed at the ends of the present-day chapters, are related via a third-person omniscient narrator. It is worth pointing out to students that in her selection of Harkryder's thoughts, McCrumb is careful never to do more than hint at the secret Spencer Arrowood has not yet learned. When Harkryder is introduced in chapter 2, his gaze lingers over a picture of his brothers, Tom and Ewell, and after twenty years in the penitentiary, he feels rage that his brothers are free. He considers recanting his confession but feels that "Nobody cared about the truth anymore."[34] Fate Harkryder and Frankie Silver's backgrounds and circumstances are so similar that when McCrumb writes, "I'm a poor, dumb hillbilly, Sheriff. Why should anybody bother to keep me alive?" a reader has to back up a few lines to see which character is speaking. Ultimately, Frankie Silver comes off as the more sympathetic of the two, and students can have a valuable discussion about how much the first-person narratives contribute to a reader's feelings for her.

Getting students to discuss McCrumb's double-barreled method should ultimately help them to understand the connections among all the major elements of narrative, to understand, for example, how the plot structure can emphasize the theme. More questions can prompt students to make these connections: Why does McCrumb yoke together the stories of Frankie Silver and Fate Harkryder? How does she structure each plot in order to emphasize the similarities? How does her selection of point of view complement the questions of guilt vs. innocence at the heart of the novel? Why does the novel end with *two* executions? In other words, why doesn't McCrumb, in the fictional plot, permit Spencer Arrowood to rescue Fate Harkryder? Why doesn't the knowledge he has

---

[34] McCrumb, *Ballad*, 60–61.

gained from figuring out Frankie Silver's story save Harkryder? What—or who—intervenes? Answering these questions will help students understand that a narrative is an orchestration of many elements, working together to produce a particular effect.

As I mentioned previously, suspense is an important element of narrative, but unraveling the plot is not the only reason readers read novels. In the case of *The Ballad of Frankie Silver*, some readers may already be familiar with details of the case from folklore or local history. Students should be asked to consider what, for these readers, is the value of McCrumb's novel. Readers commonly read narratives based on historical events, expecting authors who have conducted research to provide context and explanation. Even when readers know the facts of an event, we still want to understand why the event occurred and, if it was regrettable, how it might have been avoided or be averted in the future. This is particularly true where violence is concerned, a fact that accounts for the proliferation of the New Journalism in the 1960s. For example, Michael Herr's *Dispatches* (1977) helped explain the violence of Vietnam, John Hersey's the *Algiers Motel Incident* (1968) helped explain race-related violence, and *In Cold Blood* (1965) helped explain how violence increasingly encroached on ordinary families.[35]

Despite some disagreement about the facts of Frankie Silver's case, Sharyn McCrumb and Perry Deane Young see similar meanings in her story. For both writers, Frankie is at least as much victim as victimizer. For Young, she is the victim of poor legal strategy. Young has argued quite convincingly that when Frankie's attorney sought to get her acquitted rather than to reduce the charge to nonpremeditated murder, he made a grave mistake. Young maintains that Frankie "would have been found guilty of nothing worse than manslaughter or justifiable homicide if the details of the murder had ever been presented to the jury.... She was barred from testifying...but there was no reason [her lawyer] could not have explained to the jury that she had killed her husband in self defense."[36] Both Young and McCrumb emphasize evidence that Frankie

---

[35] Based on reporting, which began in 1968.
[36] Perry Deane Young, e-mail to the author, 6 June 2000.

was also the victim of governors who barely troubled themselves to understand her case.

Perhaps most importantly, Young and McCrumb both see Frankie as a victim of her husband, Charlie. Young says that "there were plenty of witnesses to prove he'd abused her,"[37] and McCrumb develops this thread in crafting Frankie's confession, a copy of which has never been located.[38] In McCrumb's version, Frankie emphasizes "Charlie liked to get drunk, and the liquor turned him mean."[39] The fact that the young woman probably killed her husband during a moment of real or perceived threat to herself or her child also makes her, ultimately, the victim of the state of North Carolina and of a miscarriage of justice.

In the late 1990s, a group of Morganton schoolchildren wrote to North Carolina Governor Jim Hunt, asking him to issue a pardon of forgiveness on Frankie Silver's behalf.[40] Although the pardon was denied after an investigation into the case, the schoolchildren's act demonstrates the value of teaching young people about Frankie Silver and helping them in learning to sort fact from fiction and to know the value of each.

The experience of reading Sharyn McCrumb's novel and Perry Young's book and examining original case materials can help students understand the workings of narrative, including theme, point of view, and multi-layered plots, as well as readers' differing expectations for fiction and nonfiction. Comparing primary sources against the way they may be dramatized by a fiction writer can enlighten students as to the uses of history and the difference between historical fact and literary truth or verisimilitude. And students' acquaintance with the 1830s legal system can provide them both a contrast with the present system concerning such matters as whether or not a defendant testifies on her own behalf and a comparison with contemporary events such as increased skepticism about the death penalty. Such study also reinforces the importance of active citizenship, as the Morganton citizens who

---

[37] Perry Deane Young, e-mail to the author, 6 June 2000.

[38] McCrumb, *Ballad*, 269–72.

[39] McCrumb, *Ballad,* 270.

[40] Tom Davenport, *The Ballad of Frankie Silver.* American Tradition Culture Series. In collaboration with Daniel Patterson and the University of North Carolina Curriculum in Folklore. Davenport Films, 1998.

petitioned the governor on Frankie Silver's behalf were probably, in some cases, the ancestors of the children who recently petitioned Governor Hunt.

Finally, examining *The Ballad of Frankie Silver*—or any similar work—through the method suggested here will also make students better critical readers in general, and the multimedia and multidisciplinary natures of the assignment should address another important element of education—student motivation. If studying a novel can provide such a range of benefits, then literature is very valuable, indeed.

The Lure of the Lore:

Two Hamelin Novels by Sharyn McCrumb

Anne LeCroy

"If Evelyn Waugh had written mystery stories set in the American South, he might have produced *Sick of Shadows*," remarked Fred Chappell in a review of this early novel by Sharyn McCrumb. This would be the first of the MacPherson group—I style it so because a principal character is Elizabeth MacPherson, whose life in southwest Virginia is regularly intertwined with that of close relatives living in an antebellum mansion in Georgia. The nine MacPherson novels are categorized as "the work of Jane Austen with an attitude."

McCrumb's fiction also includes two humorous, parody sci-fi novels, an early collection of stories in *Our Separate Days* (1989) and a much larger collection of short stories, *Foggy Mountain Breakdown* (1997). *Days* offers the reader of later novels—both the MacPherson novels and the Ballad Series—hints of things to come: Scots lore, characters (officers of the law especially), and glimpses of the art of the Appalachian storyteller. In the introduction to this early collection, Jim Wayne Miller writes: "Ms. McCrumb's short stories stand out as dramatizations of the conflicts between old and new ways in the southern mountains. These take place in the context of a family and between family members. There is the sinister, the bubbling humor, the obsession with family and kin, the prophetic sight and dream."[1]

It is in these stories that we find seeds of the Hamelin novels—the mulberry switch set in the ground when the new bride arrived at her home—growing over the years to a massive bush-tree; the death of the old hen that leads to the death of a brutal husband; the preacher who forbids stringed instruments as the "work of the Devil" but allows a piano, because "it's a percussion instrument;" and the sensitive, understanding sheriff.

Women from the South who have written about the southern Appalachian region are numerous: to name a few—Mary N. Murfree, Lee Smith, Harriette Arnow, and Wilma Dykeman. McCrumb is a sterling member of the group who "write because we have questions we need to examine...conflicts we need to resolve...matters we are still working through."[2] According to Ms. McCrumb whom I first met at an informal potluck in the hill country near Erwin, Tennessee, her novels draw from experience, folklore, tradition, and all the culture of the Scots-Celtic settlers in the mountains as well as of the Cherokee and Choctaw.

The Scots connection is regularly present in the MacPherson novels, which range from a small town in southwest Virginia to a small town southeast of Atlanta, to Edinburgh, a small deserted island off the west coast of Scotland, and western North Carolina. Family relationships play significant roles in these novels, too, as does some folklore and an increasingly strong sense of history; in later MacPherson novels, McCrumb weaves past and present together most effectively in a sort of mythic time cycle. There is suspense, humor, and the undercurrent of mystery, but these are not just mystery novels in which the heroine by means of pluck and luck solves the mystery. There are deaths, but they are not necessarily the focus of the reader's attention. Herbal lore, the Sight, and the elderly wise woman, conflict between past and present, the mountains and the intrusion of modern life show slightly in the early

---

[1] Sharyn McCrumb and Mona Walton Helper, *Our Separate Days* (Blacksburg VA: Rowan Mountain Press, 1989) xii.

[2] McCrumb, *Days* , xii.

novels, much more prominently in more recent novels in the series (*MacPherson's Lament* and *If I'd Killed Him When I Met Him*).

The two earliest novels in the Ballad series are the focus of my discussion in this paper. Hamelin is the town central to the action; it is surrounded by mountains of varying height and wildness and has perhaps 8500 inhabitants ranging from genteel older ladies of the book club to the dwellers in the trailer park to those who live in the mountains. Sheriff Arrowood and Nora Bonesteel—a woman with the Sight—play roles in the Ballad novels. *If Ever I Return, Pretty Peggy-O* and *The Hangman's Beautiful Daughter* go deeply into human psychology, conflicts, relationships healthy and otherwise, the spectrum of life in a community undergoing the impact of technology. This once self-sufficient community on the Little Dove River still cherishes its independence. It has traditional celebrations for Memorial Day, high school reunions, various holidays (the cycle of the Celtic year shows in *Hangman*). But it also is dependent on nearby Johnson City for a hospital and shopping; on Jonesborough for a special dinner at the Parson's Table. Knoxville is the largest city nearest Hamelin and just east of town is the North Carolina border. In other words, for one who knows something of the region, Hamelin is a type of Erwin or Hampton.

McCrumb's Ballad novels show wit and irony, careful plotting on several levels, and characters of a somewhat unique kind. These are not light romps with zany relatives, but accounts of life in Appalachia, specifically northeast Tennessee, near the Tri-Cities. The small town locale could easily be Hampton or Jonesborough. The details of scenery—mountains, meadows, streams, the river, the changing seasons—are done with the skill of an artist who has been there, lived there, and grown up there. The persons in the two novels are very real, and very fallible—the sheriff; his secretary and deputy, a Vietnam vet with deadly memories; the town eccentric; long-time inhabitants and the newcomers with jobs at nearby city industries, and the wise woman of the mountain who has the Sight—Nora Bonesteel. It is in these two novels that some materials from her own memory surface.

If Ever I Return, Pretty Peggy-O was a New York Times Notable Book in 1990 and a finalist for the Anthony and the Nero Awards. The setting, this time, is southern Appalachia, a place well known to

McCrumb who spent much time in her childhood in Erwin and knew the Tri-Cities-Erwin-Hampton-Jonesborough territory in all its seasons, its variety, its loveliness, and its harshness. The town of Hamelin in its mountain basin, close to the Little Dove River, shares its secrets, its social relationships, and its complex characters with the reader who may well conclude this novel reluctantly and deeply affected.

The opening is Memorial Day, when Sheriff Spencer Arrowood visits his brother Cal's grave in the local cemetery to reverence it by pouring a bottle of beer over it and recalling the Vietnam War that caused Cal's death. Cal had been the big man of the family and of the school; Spencer had always been bullied by him and walked in his shadow. And that shadow treads through the novel, along with others, especially the lingering effects of those years in Indochina and the pain that still strikes such veterans as Deputy Joe LeDonne and Baby Boomers such as Peggy Muryan, once a popular folksinger of the 1960s.

But there is also a high school twentieth class reunion to plan for and the usual business of the town. Strange threatening postcards reach Peggy and we are presented with letters from Vietnam between every few chapters, from the man Peggy once shared her gig with but dropped when the big time called her but didn't want him. The days pass and odd things happen; suspects prove innocent, threads of plot begin to wind together, never obviously or through forced coincidence. No one is free of some guilt in the past; characters are complex—there is no ostensible villain, no clear-cut hero. Jane Arrowood's thoughts give a fairly clear picture of the situation:

> It was only men who thought that everything was cut-and-dried, black-and-white. The older Jane got the more she seemed to see ambiguity in everything...she would settle for understanding things... She wondered, sometimes, if her men folks thought her stupid. Perhaps so; they were not likely to see that there could be other forms of wisdom besides their own... She saw life as a field of tangled kudzu vines, with endless runners going in all directions beneath the surface. In her mind

she wanted to unearth the kudzu and examine the roots, to find the hidden connections between people and events.[3]

Spencer's days involve him in minor breaches of the law—a man importing raccoons from Ohio for the local hunters; underage drinkers; graveyard foolishness by a few kids. The reunion is always looming over him, along with the memory of his former wife—especially now that he is interested in Peggy. The denouement is credible, realistic, and hard to put out of one's mind—there is the feeling "this could easily have happened, here, not long ago."

Descriptions abound in the Ballad novels. I offer one:

> There were just enough clouds in the sky to make the town look like a postcard. Buffalo Mountain seemed to curl around the valley, shielding Hamelin from the expanse of sky and from any view of the rest of Tennessee. To get out of Wake County, Spencer's father used to say, you had to sneak past the mountains: on the two-lane black top that wound around the mountain like a corkscrew; on Cade's Creek which snaked through the valley and underground before it joined the river in the next county; or on the Appalachian Trail, which threaded its way through the hills and fields...to stay out of Wake County was even harder; then you had to get the mountains out of you. Most people never managed it. Spencer...didn't think that anything a high salary would buy could compensate him for the loss of these mountains.[4]

Later, Spencer takes Peggy to see the ancestral Arrowood home place, back in Pigeon Creek. "When I come up into these hollers, I feel like I'm taking a time machine instead of a car," he tells Peggy.

This past—Vietnam, memories of high school hurts and worries, failed marriages, family misunderstandings, and a nostalgia that misfires

---

[3] Sharyn McCrumb, *If Ever I Return, Pretty Peggy-O* (New York: Ballantine, 1990) 221–22.

[4] McCrumb, *Peggy-O*, 106–107.

and causes anguish and death—points to the old saying that "those who try to forget the past are condemned to repeat it." This could well be the epigraph for the entire novel.

Reviews praise the novel as a "quantum leap forward…a superior mystery, surpassing earlier novels…she made us laugh in her other novels, moved us with this one." The humor of the MacPherson books is still there, but subdued, wry, striking suddenly as part of life, mixing with pathos, pain, and love.

The *Hangman's Beautiful Daughter*, using many of the same characters and the same setting focuses on the events in the lives of four women: Laura Bruce, Maggie Underhill, Nora Bonesteel, and—very briefly—Tammy Robsart. An ever-present figure in the novel is the Little Dove River, which flows, brown, dead, dun-colored through the valley carrying waste from Titan Paper Company in North Carolina.[5] And the mountains, with their changing shadows, their old, winding roads, their abandoned cabins nestle the town. "Why can't we get out of these hills?" wonders Spencer, as he looks at the children gathered to receive goodies thrown from the Santa train. "Why are we willing to sacrifice so much to live in this beautiful place?"[6]

Like *Peggy-O, Daughter* is more than a mystery, a series of violent acts to be resolved; it is the saga or epic of three seasons in the life of a town and its kaleidoscope of citizens, the folklore and song of the Appalachians, the atmosphere of those mountains of which a character in the story "Telling the Bees" said, "These mountains don't stand back and pose and show off [like the Rockies]. The Appalachians come close and hold you." The humor is still there, natural humor in the talk and some of the actions of the townspeople. There is no satire, no condescension. The people of the town are strong, able to endure, sometimes querulous, sometimes petulant—very human.

Laura puts in words an important theme in this second ballad novel— "It was just like God to let the trained professional in His service

---

[5] Sharyn McCrumb, *The Hangman's Beautiful Daughter* (New York: Scribners, 1992) 14.
[6] McCrumb, *Hangman*, 140–41.

sit around and then draft a complete amateur to do the job."[7] Though this thought comes near the conclusion of the *Hangman's Beautiful Daughter*, it could be a thesis for this second novel set in Hamelin where Spencer Arrowood and Joe LeDonne work to keep the town peaceable, while the town eccentric parades each day in a different costume (now Ninja Turtle, now Batman, now Robin Hood), the citizens celebrate the seasons from Thanksgiving to Easter in various ways, family violence erupts, and we see the poverty of the town as well as the middle-class prosperity, thanks to nearby industry. Taw and Tavy, two old fishing buddies now back together, incite action against a polluting industry up the Little Dove River. A mysterious stranger moves into the woods, upsetting LeDonne more than he feels he should be. Laura, the wife of the local minister (who is now serving for clean-up work for Desert Storm), tries to fit her suburban Roanoke culture into the Appalachian way of life as she awaits their first child. And above all is the mysterious Nora Bonesteel, a woman with the Sight, a healer, and a wise confidante.

After Christmas, true winter settles in and the dark undersides of the town keep surfacing to Spencer, to Laura, to Taw and Tavy, and to Maggie, left orphan with her brother Mark after a violent family disruption. It is cold and dark—as Appalachia can be—and folk memory, Celtic-Scots memory, stirs in the novel. Spring brings torrential rains and a flood of the lowlands—and a settlement of many things. Life goes on—happy, sad, forlorn, blissful—but little things show too. Nora's elderly groundhog Persey (for Persephone) comes out of hibernation; the chestnut survives. The community gathers at Shiloh Church to share Easter services.

Not a murder mystery, really, nor in any sense a detective novel, *Hangman* is like the long chronicle of an historian of the year—or most of it—who tells history through people and conversations and thoughts. The element of myth includes the triple goddess, Maggie, Laura, Nora; Persephone; and the floodwaters of baptism and death. Almost like an epilogue to the novel is this piece from the *Johnson City Press:* "For years, the Pigeon River has been a sore spot for Tennesseans who claimed that a North Carolina paper mill was polluting it beyond use. But

---

[7] McCrumb, *Hangman*, 285.

a 330 million dollar modernization of the Champion International Corp. mill in Canton, North Carolina has made headway in cleaning up the river for rafting, fishing, swimming."

Sharyn McCrumb's Use of Ballads in

If Ever I Return, Pretty Peggy-O

Danny L. Miller

Sharyn McCrumb's early comic novels (*Bimbos of the Death Sun* and *Zombies of the Gene Pool*) and her Elizabeth MacPherson novels have given way in recent years to her Ballad series, as she and readers call this series of novels set in east Tennessee which take their titles from old ballads and folksongs and have Sheriff Spencer Arrowood as their general main character. McCrumb herself sees these novels as her best work. She says, "It's what I always wanted to write. When I was a graduate student my focus was on Appalachian literature and culture so I studied and got more deeply into the culture."[1] Indeed, it is the greatest strength of these novels that they are foremost about the Appalachian culture and people. As Meredith Sue Willis states: "One of the great pleasures of reading these books is that a character whose consciousness is the main point of view in one book becomes in the next—or even in another passage in the same novel—part of the local color. This varied and shifting point of view allows McCrumb to make the real star of the Ballad series not any single individual but the region itself."[2] "While the

---

[1] Charles Silet, "She Walks These Hills: An Interview with Sharyn McCrumb" *The Armchair Detective* 28/4 (Fall 1995): 375.

[2] Meredith Sue Willis, "The Ballads of Sharyn McCrumb" *Appalachian Journal* 25/3 (Spring 1998): 320.

[Elizabeth] MacPherson books start with a plot," McCrumb says, "the Ballad books start with themes" and these themes very often relate to Appalachian culture.[3]

That these novels (*If Ever I Return, Pretty Peggy-O, The Hangman's Beautiful Daughter, She Walks These Hills, The Rosewood Casket, The Ballad of Frankie Silver*, and *The Songcatcher*) are called a "Ballad Series" points to some kind of connection in the minds of readers (and the author herself) between them and the Scottish, English and Appalachian ballads, and indeed there is a connection. Beginning with the first of these, *If Ever I Return, Pretty Peggy-O*, the title of which comes from the traditional Scottish folksong "Fennario," McCrumb utilizes the old ballads and folksongs in several ways to help shape, unify, and enrich the novel.

First, the ballads are used to form a soundtrack (backdrop) for *Peggy*, helping to create the atmosphere; this atmosphere is kind of a folk revival 1960s mingled with suspenseful foreboding. One can almost hear the ballads and folksongs while reading the novel. Music, in general, plays a strong role in *Peggy*, as it does in McCrumb's own personal life. Says McCrumb of the creative influence of music on her own writing: "Music is a continuous wellspring of creativity for me. When I was writing the subsequent Appalachian Ballad novels [after *Peggy*], I would make a sound track for each book, before I began the actual process of writing. The cassette tape, dubbed by me from tracks of albums in my extensive collection, would contain songs that I felt were germane to the themes of the book...."[4] Throughout *Peggy*, dozens of 1960s folksingers are mentioned—Pete Seeger; Buffy St. Marie; Peter, Paul, and Mary; Ian and Sylvia; and, of course, Joan Baez, the obvious prototype for Peggy Muryan the folksinger in the novel. Likewise, many other musicians are mentioned: the Everly Brothers, the Statler Brothers, and Elvis of course, to name just a few.

Spencer Arrowood is described: "As compensation for the lack of an AM-FM radio in his patrol car, Spencer had developed an automatic

---

[3] Silet, "Interview," 371.
[4] Sharyn McCrumb, "Keepers of the Legends," www.sharynmccrumb.com, 30 April 2003.

Muzak in his mind."[5] And throughout the novel, in his head Spencer plays an appropriate soundtrack of songs to accompany the action: "Without his conscious thought, his mind would provide a continuous background hum of popular songs to entertain him while he drove. Sometimes, he'd noticed, he could tell how he felt about something by analyzing the songs going through his head: "Good Day, Sunshine" meant a good mood; "I'm Looking Through You" told him that he was pissed off. The songs were seldom of a later vintage than 1970...."[6]

Although his repertoire is pre-1970, Spencer knows some of the old ballads as well, mainly as a result of the 1960s folksong revival (or as some of my musician friends call it, the "folksong scare"). The prototype of Spencer in this regard may have been McCrumb's own father. She says of him: "I had loved folk music when I was in college, and I had grown up listening to my father's mixture of Ernest Tubb and Francis Child."[7] And elsewhere she states, "...my father would sing...I got a combination of modern country music and old ballads brought over from England."[8]

The folksong revival of the 1960s provided a link between the almost forgotten and certainly fast disappearing Scottish, English, and Appalachian ballads of the late nineteenth and early twentieth centuries and the present. Spencer Arrowood even refers to this link between the past and the present in *Peggy* when he tells Peggy Muryan, the folksinger who has come to live in Hamelin, Tennessee, about learning to play the guitar as a teenager and singing "A Fair Young Maid, All in the Garden" (which he has learned from a Joan Baez record). While he was learning to play the song, Spencer's father came in and joined him:

John Riley.' Peggy nodded, recognizing the line. Right. From the very latest Joan Baez album. Now I knew that my dad was not into the counterculture, and he didn't know Joan Baez

---

[5] Sharyn McCrumb, *If Ever I Return, Pretty Peggy-O* (New York: Ballantine 1990) 16.

[6] McCrumb, *Peggy-O*, 16.

[7] McCrumb, "Keepers."

[8] Sharyn McCrumb, "A Novelist Looks at the Southern Mountains," www.sharynmccrumb.com, 30 April 2003.

from Betty Crocker, so how come he knows my new song?'
'New song.' Peggy smiled. 'Four hundred years old.' 'Yeah. He
said he'd heard it from his grandmother. Mary of the riding crop.
His tune was all wrong—sounded like Ernest Tubb—but he was
letter perfect on the words.'[9]

Most of us, like Spencer, if we know folksongs or ballads at all, do so
because of the 1960s, which served as a link between the far away past
and the ever-changing present.

The link between the present and the past is symbolized by the
focus on and use of the old ballads in *Peggy-O*, which helps to reveal a
major theme in McCrumb's novels: the relationship between past and
present. In almost all of the Ballad novels (certainly *The Hangman's
Beautiful Daughter, The Rosewood Casket,* and *The Ballad of Frankie
Silver*) events in the present are paralleled by events of the past as
characters in the present try to make sense of their contemporary lives.
When asked in an interview, "Would you care to comment on your sense
of history and the role of history in our lives today?" McCrumb
answered, "In *The Rosewood Casket* I use as an epigraph the Pinero
quote, 'The future is the past, entered through another door.' Anybody
who deals with Southern literature concludes that you can't make sense
of anything without the past to provide context."[10] Surely, the present
setting of McCrumb's novels are very "modern" Appalachia, not the
quaint and/or unusual nor the romanticized picture (folksy craftspeople)
we often think of, but a realistic picture of people living in the mountains
today. As one review says, "Her Appalachia is not…filled with lovable
comic characters or gothics from *Deliverance*. The people who live in
Hamelin, Tennessee, are different because they have remained connected
with their past, their history, but are not reconciled with it."[11] There
certainly is a small town flavor to the novels, but most people are not
isolated in hollers (although some *are*)—they go to restaurants, to malls

---

[9] McCrumb, *Peggy-O*, 60.
[10] McCrumb, "Novelist."
[11] Sharon A. Russell, "Sharyn McCrumb." In *Great Women Mystery Writers:
Classic to Contemporary,* ed. Kathleen Gregory Klein (Westport CT: Greenwood Press,
1994) 201.

in nearby cities, etc., and they are increasingly victims of crime. But there are certain qualities of Appalachian life that McCrumb presents that have not changed—such as the connection to the past (through oral storytelling) or care for/about the elderly.

Even today (when Appalachians have become so homogenized with the rest of the country through television, etc.) the link between past and present is one aspect of culture that keeps Appalachia somewhat unique. Families still go to graveyard decorations or family reunions, and they are surrounded by the past—pieces of furniture that belonged to great-grandparents or even the "old homeplace" itself (which becomes like a shrine to them). In the fast-paced, "modern" Appalachian world that McCrumb depicts, she still manages to achieve an awareness of and legacy of the past (both personal for her characters and cultural for the region). "Hamelin, Tennessee," she writes in *If Ever I Return, Pretty Peggy-O*, "was still bound by traditions, even when the meanings had been obscured by time."[12] And many of those traditions (certainly representing values, such as patriotism and familism) are at the heart of Appalachian culture.

In addition to providing background atmosphere/music and thematic connections in the novel, McCrumb uses the ballads and folksongs as a unifying device. The messages sent to Peggy are all in the form of the ballads. The first threatening note, for example, reads: "IS LITTLE MARGARET IN THE HOUSE, OR IS SHE IN THE HALL?"[13] From the old English ballad "Little Margaret." Peggy explains the note's allusion to Spencer:

It's [the song] about a revenant. That's a folklore term. Little Margaret's lover marries someone else, and she shows up on his wedding night, but when he goes to her house to find her—that's when this line comes in. He says: "Is Little Margaret in the house or is she in the hall?" And her people answer him:

---

[12] McCrumb, *Peggy-O*, 9.
[13] McCrumb, *Peggy-O*, 57.

"Little Margaret's sleeping in her coal-black coffin, with her face to the wall."[14]

So it was Little Margaret's ghost who visited the former lover, and this adds a note of supernaturalism to the atmosphere of the novel. Later in the novel, Peggy receives another message written in the lines of the ballad "Knoxville Girl:" "I TOOK HER BY HER GOLDEN HAIR,/ I THROWED HER ROUND AND ROUND."[15] In addition, many of the epigraphs of the chapters are also lines from ballads, adding another level of unity to the novel.

Another connection between the ballads and the novel is the subject matter. Certainly, a great many of the ballads are "murder ballads," in which women are victimized and killed by men for a variety of reasons. The murder ballads are among the most well known sub-genre of ballads. Ballads are above all narrative poems that tell a good story—and this is an obvious parallel with McCrumb's novels: she too tells a good story. The theme of the Scottish folksong "Fennario" also relates to the theme of the novel—both could be said to be about unrequited love. "Fennario" is in the tradition of "Barbara Ellen," in which the lady witholds her love from the man and he dies of grief, rather than the murder ballads in which women are killed. Because of missing pertinent information, the Joan Baez version of this traditional Scottish folksong is difficult to decipher, but other versions are more comprehendible:

As we marched out to Fennario
As we marched out to Fennario
Our captain fell in love with a lady like a dove
And the name she was called was pretty Peggy-O

Won't you come and go with me, pretty Peggy-O
Won't you come and go with me, pretty Peggy-O
In coaches you shall ride with your true love by your side
Just as grand as any lady in the are-O

[14] McCrumb, *Peggy-O*, 58.
[15] McCrumb, *Peggy-O*, 158.

What would your mother think, pretty Peggy-O?
What would your mother think, pretty Peggy-O?
What would your mother think for to hear the guineas clink
And the soldiers all marching before you?

You're the man that I adore, sweet William-O
You're the man that I adore, sweet William-O
You're the man that I adore, but your fortune is too low
I'm afraid that my mother would be angry-O

Come tripping down the stairs, pretty Peggy-O
Come tripping down the stairs, pretty Peggy-O
Come tripping down the stairs and tie up your yellow hair
Bid a last farewell to sweet William-O

If ever I return, pretty Peggy-O
If ever I return, pretty Peggy-O
If ever I return then the city I shall burn
And destroy all the ladies in the are-O

Our captain he is dead, pretty Peggy-O
Our captain he is dead, pretty Peggy-O
Our captain he is dead, and he died for a maid
And he's buried in Louisiana country-O.

In "Fennario," Pretty Peggy-O will not go away with the captain, Sweet William, because he is too poor, and thus, after they have bade farewell, William threatens to return and seek revenge: "If ever I return all your cities I will burn/Destroying all the ladies in the are-O." Similarly, Travis's love for Peggy is unrequited, thus setting him up as the murderer (the returning destroyer). There is also a suggestion of war in "Fennario," which relates to the Vietnam war theme in the novel. In "Fennario" the soldiers are marching into town and their captain falls in love with pretty Peggy-O. Spencer's brother Cal, Travis Perdue, Joe LeDonne, and Roger Gabriel all served in the Vietnam War. Pix-Kyle

Weaver is obsessed with the war and executes many of his actions in military fashion (ritualistic killings, etc.).

As well as using the ballads to create atmosphere, help unify the novel, and suggest some of the major subjects and themes, McCrumb tells us about the genre of the old ballads throughout *Peggy*. As Meredith Sue Willis says: "McCrumb is old-fashioned in another admirable way as well. A hundred years ago, the common reader usually expected to be informed as well as entertained, and McCrumb believes in teaching her readers. Her books are full of details about everything...."[16] The ballads are indeed an historical part of the Appalachian culture, and McCrumb wants to educate her readers by providing details and information about the ballads and their history.

One of the things I respond to most positively about McCrumb's use of the ballads as a foregrounding for her Appalachian novels is the democratic nature of the ballads—ballads were not "literature" in an elitist sense, but were the entertainment of the people—they were "popular" not in the sense of being well-known and liked (although they were) but in being "of the populace." Writing in *English and Scottish Popular Ballads* by Helen Child Sargent (daughter of Francis James Child) and noted Anglo-Saxon scholar George Lyman Kittredge state, for example: "History, as we understand it, is the written record or even the printed volume; it is no longer the accumulated fund of tribal memories, handed down from father to son by oral tradition. Yet everybody knows that, quite apart from what we usually call literature, there is a great mass of song and story and miscellaneous lore which circulates among those who have neither books nor newspapers."[17]

"To this oral literature, as the French call it," Sargent and Kittredge continue, "education is no friend. Culture destroys it, sometimes with amazing rapidity:" "when a nation learns to read, it begins to disregard its traditional tales; it feels a little ashamed of them; and finally it loses both the will and the power to remember and transmit them. What was once the possession of the folk as a whole, becomes the heritage of the

---

[16] Willis, "Ballads," 322.
[17] Helen Child Sargent and George Lyman Kittredge, *English and Scottish Popular Ballads* (Boston: Houghton Mifflin, 1904) xii.

illiterate only, and soon, unless it is gathered up by the antiquary, vanishes altogether."[18] As Sargent and Kittredge assert, the ballads "are not, like written literature, the exclusive possession of the cultivated classes in any community. They belonged, in the first instance, to the whole people, at a time when there were no formal divisions of literate and illiterate; when the intellectual interests of all were substantially identical, from the king to the peasant."[19] Part of my personal interest in the ballads is that they were a communal and oral production that was "of the people," not the "sophisticated" (and educated) classes. As a scholar, I am most interested in the "folk" or common entertainment versus the "elitist" and "high-brow." I personally detest the "high modernism" of the twentieth century, for example. And this relates to my appreciation of Appalachia in general—that what we often devalue in society is the "humble" or "folk" over the "sophisticated." So much of popular literature today is devalued by the literati or the scholarly establishment because it is "popular," and yet this literature reaches a large (and not unsophisticated) audience. Even Meredith Sue Willis seems to disparagingly dismiss McCrumb in some ways by her offhand comment, "McCrumb is of course a popular writer."[20]

Sharyn McCrumb utilizes ballads in several ways in *Peggy*. Phrases and situations from the ballads help to create a certain atmosphere of mystery and suspense. McCrumb uses phrases from the ballads and other folksongs as epigraphs to chapters, as the texts of threatening messages in the book, and as subjects of discussion among characters, helping to create a sense of unity in the novel. Throughout the novel, McCrumb refers to old ballads, many of them related to the folksong revival of the 1960s, but she often refers to the Child ballads and other ballad scholars such as Basom Lamar Lunsford of Asheville, North Carolina. Surely, it is not a misnomer to refer to these books by Sharyn McCrumb as a "Ballad Series."

[18] Sargent, "English and Scottish," xii.
[19] Sargent, "English and Scottish," xii.
[20] Willis, "Ballads," 327.

The Art of Sharyn McCrumb:

Anthropologist and Balladeer

Susan Wittig Albert

One of the interesting changes taking place in contemporary American mainstream and popular fiction is the increasing number of regional novels that are published each year. Commercial publishing being what it is, this growth is in part a response to editors' and readers' preferences. But it also arises out of the desire of writers to resist the McDonaldization of American culture by focusing on the particularities, the individual qualities of a region. Or they may have a compelling wish to preserve the history of a place or a people, or to explore its rich folk literature, now in danger of being eroded by mass-market entertainment.

Sharyn McCrumb, whose growing body of work marks her as a writer of emerging significance, turns to the regional novel because she sees how urgent it is that we recognize what is around us before it has disappeared, eroded by the commercialization of our culture, leveled by Network English, or normalized by "national standards." In *She Walks These Hills*, the third book in her "Ballad Series," she shows us these forces for change in Appalachia, and weighs them against the allure of the tragic past and the enticement of home; that place, the root of the heart, that is most particular, and most unchanged. Writing with a sure, strong sense of place, she initiates us into the deepest mysteries of home and heart and offers us an Appalachian novel that is at once a celebration and a requiem. She does this from two perspectives: from the objective, "outer" viewpoint of the anthropologist, and from the inner viewpoint of the artist.

The Art of the Anthropologist

From the anthropological references scattered throughout her books, it is clear that McCrumb reads widely in the field of anthropology. In one of her books, the main character, Elizabeth MacPherson, is a forensic anthropologist. In the dedication of *If Ever I Return, Pretty Peggy-O,* (the first book in the Ballad series,) she calls herself a bricoleur, a term used by Levi-Strauss to describe someone who cobbles together odds and ends of old things, retaining their forms and their special characteristics while creating something strikingly new, something unique and different. And in *She Walks These Hills*, she describes history graduate student Jeremy Cobb as being "betwixt and between," the title of a book by anthropologist Victor Turner that describes the experience of passage.[1] On the same page, she refers to Turner's idea of "liminality: an ecstatic condition of mind, ritually induced, in which the individual is particularly susceptible to the mysterious forces of the natural and supernatural worlds. In all her books, McCrumb demonstrates an anthropologist's understanding of myth; we tell ourselves stories to explain who we are and how we got that way.

To describe McCrumb's art, I'd like to borrow two concepts from the French structural anthropologist, Claude Levi-Strauss. According to Levi-Strauss, the basic form of prose narrative is linear, or diachronic. A narrative, especially one that is built around a strong plot, moves through time with a compelling forward energy, like a melody, one note following another. The writer may construct multiple plots or use flashbacks, or she may tell the story from different points of view,

---

[1] Sharyn McCrumb, *She Walks These Hills* (New York: Scribners, 1994) 251.

altering the forward movement. But one of the most powerful moments of narrative—perhaps the most powerful movement—is the diachronic pull, tugging the reader through the unfolding story. According to Levi-Strauss, however, there is another kind of structure, most often found in myth, which he calls synchrony. If diachronic patterns are like simple melodies, moving across time, synchronic patterns are like complex harmonies—chord structures produced by multiple, blended voices, none of which are dominant. Myth and folktales, with their repetitions and redundancies, are strongly synchronic. So is lyric poetry; echoing metaphors, rhymes, and rhythms thwart our forward movement through the poem, pulling us back again and again to its central concept, its emotional core. While *She Walks These Hills* is constructed with a diachronic thrust that compels us forward through the plot, it is also built synchronically, like a folktale, like a poem, like a ballad.

The Art of the Balladeer

As the term "Ballad Series" suggests the narrative form of McCrumb's mystery is also the poetic form of a folk ballad. Ballads are long poems built of short stanzas with a great deal of repetition, designed to make sure the audience can't miss the central idea; if the story is not understood in one way or at one level, it will be understood at another. Ballad stanzas are often organized in units something like the chapters in a book, each of which is built on a particular motif or theme and usually has a common rhyming pattern or pattern of linked words. (This kind of organization is probably related to the oral origins of the ballad. In past centuries, ballad-makers composed their songs aloud; the rhyme may have been a key to holding long segments of story in their memories.)

The structure of *She Walks These Hills* is very simple, built out of the familiar folktale motifs of the hero's escape from captivity and the journey home. But the novel achieves an extraordinary complexity as the writer repeats these motifs in different ways and at different levels in the interwoven stories of seven people, each a hero in his or her own ballad. When we set out the basic outlines of the characters' stories, their relationships become clearer and we see how each individual narrative replicates, ballad-fashion, the central statement of the novel: that the fundamental mystery of life is a journey into the personal past and the past of the community, a "journey of revelations" into the depths of the human heart.

In 1780, pregnant Katie Wyler is captured by Shawnee. She gives birth, then kills her child in order to escape her captivity. She journeys home through the Appalachian wilderness but on her arrival is murdered by the baby's father, enraged at her betrayal. Her spirit lingers as the "woman who walks the hills."

Graduate student and "seeker of knowledge" Jeremy Cobb plans to earn his Ph.D. with a dissertation on Katie Wyler. He leaves the university to follow her path through the wilderness. The journey is an initiation for this "pasteurized, climate-controlled, mobilized product of a softer era" into the savage mystery of the wilderness, as well as an initiation into his profession as an historian, the teller of other people's stories.[2]

Teen-aged Sabrina is a Melungeon ("an olive-skinned people of uncertain origin who had lived in the northeast Tennessee mountains for generations") who marries a Harkryder boy and finds herself a captive in the Harkryder's mountain compound.[3] Like Katie, Sabrina kills her baby in order to escape. "I just had to get away from there…I felt like a prisoner have to stay trapped up there in painter Cove, missing my own people…I thought if I could just get shut of this kid, things could go back to being like they was before, and I'd be free to leave."[4]

Sixty-three-year-old Harm Sorley is afflicted with Korsakoff's Syndrome and is "stuck" in memory in the 1960s. He escapes from prison and walks fifty miles home through the

---

[2] McCrumb, *Walks*, 62.
[3] McCrumb, *Walks*, 79.
[4] McCrumb, *Walks*, 318.

wilderness, only to rush to his death in his burning former home. The Sorleys are "part of the vivid old days;" as Nora Bonesteel remembers: "They sailed through dust on washboard roads in their battered black coupes; costarred in every court docket posted in the county; and swaggered their way into oblivion, leaving a trail of blood and broken hearts in their wake. Harm was the last of them…she would hate to see him go."[5]

Harm's ex-wife Rita leaves the respectability of her prison-like second marriage ("spending her life being grateful and walking a social chalkline") to search for Harm. Upon her return to their abandoned trailer home, she is murdered by her second husband, enraged at her faithlessness.[6]

Hank the Yank, a "carpetbagger from Connecticut," is a radio talk show host who becomes deeply involved with Harm's escape and convinced that Harm was unjustly imprisoned and should be redeemed. In his investigation, he goes to Harm and Rita's abandoned trailer home, where he finds Rita's body.

Martha Ayers is a newly appointed deputy who plans to capture Harm as "her ticket to a permanent position as deputy" and to earn the respect of her lover, Deputy Joe LeDonne. Martha's search, like Jeremy's wilderness journey, is an initiation into the mystery of her own nature and into her relationship with her lover, as well as her profession as a law officer.

The journey of these characters teaches us something about the homeward, backward, inward journey that each of us must make. It is a mythic journey, the stuff of ballads and folktales that defines us as individuals and as members of the human family. In this journey, we must meet the wilderness as it is, discarding anything that separates us

---

[5] McCrumb, *Walks*, 2.
[6] McCrumb, *Walks*, 5.

from it. This is part of what Jeremy learns, for instance, as he discards bit by bit pieces of the camping equipment he had assembled to make his journey easier: the "burden of over-civilized existence."

Journeying through the wilderness is perilous enough, but arrival is even more dangerous, and often tragic. As Katie whispers to Harm, "You don't want to go home," because, she knows, death waits there.[7] But later, sadly, she tells him: "I reckon we have to go home."[8] Home is the point from which all journeys begin and the point where they end. Home is where we are born and where we die, birth and death "one with death rising to bloom again," as in the elegiac poem by James Still that opens the novel. We don't want to go home, but we have to.

The ballad structure of *She Walks These Hills* is evident not only in the interwoven, replicative plots based on the motif of the homeward journey, but also in the organization of the chapters themselves. Each of the eighteen chapters is divided into sections, like ballad stanzas, each told from a different point of view, using different poetic devices.

One poetic device that McCrumb borrows from the ballad is the stanzaic form. The similarity of her chapter sections to ballad stanzas, built on repeated rhyme, metaphor, and motif, is often quite striking. Chapter 4, for example, is divided into four sections. In the first section, novice policewoman Martha Ayers talks to Sheriff Spencer Arrowood about outfitting herself with a new gun and a Kevlar vest; the sheriff, instructing the novice, tells her that as a beginner she needs to stick to easy things—serving warrants, escorting funerals, typing reports. In section two, Jeremy Cobb goes to a sporting goods store to outfit himself for his hiking trip. The salesclerk, an experienced hiker, tells him that he needs to stick to the "easy beginner trails." In the third section, Martha's instruction is continued as she learns about outlaws; the sheriff tells her the story of Harm's uncle, Dalton Sorley, a handsome renegade outlaw and ballad hero who escaped from prison several times and was caught going home. In the fourth section, Hank the Yank is instructed in the ways of outlaws. Vaguely understanding that Harm Sorley is the "last of something," he goes to the local newspaper to research the murder for

---

[7] MCCrumb, *Walks*, 203.
[8] McCrumb, *Walks*, 241.

which Harm was tried in 1968. He finds out the basic elements of Harm's story, which closely parallels Dalton Sorley's outlawry. Hank's and Martha's task, and the reader's, too, is to learn through Harm something of what he represents: a declining vividness, a kind of lawless wildness that is no longer at home in the tamer world of modern civilization: "Harm added the spice of manageable danger to an increasingly civilized segment of mountain wilderness. Sure, we have Japanese restaurants and tanning salons, Johnson City people could tell visitors, but there are still bears and rattlesnakes in the woods, and even an escaped mountain man at large: old but still too tough and wily for the law to catch."[9]

Another poetic device McCrumb uses to organize her chapters is the chapter headnote, which introduces a major idea or plot element that will be explored in each of the chapter's sections. She used this same technique in earlier books in the series, taking the headnotes from a variety of sources. In *She Walks These Hills*, the headnotes come from hymns.[10] The head note to chapter 1, for instance, lays out the entire chapter's essential elements: "My Lord calls me, He calls me by the lightning;/ The trumpet sounds within my soul: I have not long to stay here/ Steal away, steal away home."

---

[9] McCrumb, *Walks*, 70.

[10] McCrumb not only uses music to establish theme and set mood for her readers, she uses it for herself in the composing process. In a 26 December 1994 letter to the author, she writes, "When I am doing a scene from the point of view of a particular character, I play music related to that character. Not necessarily music that I like, but music that the character listens to, or that defines him. (Example: for Joe LeDonne, the soundtrack is always 60s acid music: the Grateful Dead, the Doors; for Spencer, I play intellectual country: Don Williams, the Statler Brothers, Kris Kristofferson.) So 'ballads' really are an integral part of the narrative to the extent that each book has a 'sound track.' For *She Walks These Hills*, the play list includes: 'The Long Black Veil,' 'Jamie Raeburn,' (an obscure Scottish folk song—that and 'Fox on the Run' are Harm's theme songs), 'Better Class of Losers' (Randy Travis), 'The Renegade' and 'Someday Soon' (Ian Tyson), 'The Hobo's Meditation' (Jimmie Rodgers), 'The Bounty Hunter' (Mike Cross), etc. And, of course, the hymns mentioned in the text. I actually made a tape of these songs, and I played it over at least a hundred times, usually when I was making long drives alone, trying to internalize all these messages, because it's the only way I can carry all these people around in my head simultaneously."

In the chapter's first section, Harm Sorley receives a message from the Lord: "The lightning flashed again, and the rumble of the thunder seemed nearer this time. Harm knew it was the Lord, urging him on…And his feet itched. Itching feet mean you are going on a journey."[11] From here on, the revelations don't come in the lightning and thunder, but through more ordinary communication channels. In section two, the sheriff's office receives a fax from the Correctional Center at Mountain City, reporting Harm's escape—his effort to "steal away home." In section three, Hank the Yank, reading the news on WHTN, gets the message of Harm's escape off the newswire, along with all the other "boring" news of the day. In section four, Nora Bonesteel gets the news from WHTN, bringing the chapter full circle and home: "On Ashe Mountain Nora Bonesteel switched off her radio, and stood staring out at the blue ripple of mountains that stretched away from the edge of her meadow…So Harm was out, and homeward bound."[12] The motif of the first chapter headnote is echoed in the last, from *Amazing Grace*: "Through many dangers, toils and snares, I have already come:/ 'Tis grace has brought me safe thus far,/ And grace will lead me home."

A third poetic device in this book is the repetition of major ideas, like *time* and *history*, which mean different things to different characters. Harm, for instance, suffers from a memory disorder that fixes him in time. In prison, he lives in "zap time;"[13] after he escapes, Hank says, he's traveling through "the Twilight Zone."[14] "You may get this Harm fellow out of the hills," Dr. Caudill tells Joe LeDonne, "but you'll never get him out of the past."[15] The *Hamelin County Record* is "like a time capsule," according to its editor, "but it's sundial time: they count no hours but unclouded ones."[16] Ethnohistorian Jeremy Cobb is obsessed with the time of the eighteenth-century Katie Wyler's: "he had almost willed it to be 1779. Katie's time."[17] Hank the Yank (whose first song in the book is

---

[11] McCrumb, *Walks*, 9–10.
[12] McCrumb, *Walks*, 17–18.
[13] McCrumb, *Walks*, 8.
[14] McCrumb, *Walks*, 191.
[15] McCrumb, *Walks*, 42.
[16] McCrumb, *Walks*, 74.
[17] McCrumb, *Walks*, 251.

"Tomorrow Never Comes") sees himself as the "official historian of Harm Sorley," determined to find out what really happened in 1968, when Hank killed Claib Maggard.[18] The keeper of documents at the county courthouse where he does research is reading (in one of the marvelous little inside jokes that pepper all McCrumb's books) *A Brief History of Time*. And Nora Bonesteel, who has seen Katie Wyler running through the hills, knows that her own perception of time and history is remarkably different from other people's, giving her an ability to live in the past, the present, and the future at once: "Most folks see only what is here and now, but she [Nora] could see what was and what was going to be."[19]

As in a ballad, McCrumb plays out her motifs in both major and minor keys. The ambiguous motif of *honor*, for instance, underlies much of the book. Honor is almost always coupled with a kind of hypermasculinity ("macho games," the sheriff calls it) and with violence. As a woman and as a law officer, Martha Ayers sees the danger in a culture where honor and guns breed death.

> Some Southern men seemed to feel that Appomatox was the last insult their manhood would ever suffer. They fought authority at every turn; met every slight with clenched fists; and died to prove how brave they were. Some of them were outlaws, and some of them were cops. But almost all of them were male, and Martha thought that all of them were crazy. Gallant, romantic, quixotic, courageous—maybe all of those things—but doubly dangerous for all that, and no less crazy.[20]

Martha's insight into the ambiguity of honor is underscored by the death of Patrick Allen, who shoots himself because he has lost his girlfriend to another boy, wrecked his car while driving drunk, and disappointed his parents' expectation of their honor student, Eagle Scout son. It is also understood by Joe LeDonne's masculine reaction to

[18] McCrumb, *Walks*, 36.
[19] McCrumb, *Walks*, 2.
[20] McCrumb, *Walks*, 172–73.

Martha's new job as deputy: "I didn't realize," he says in a moment of insight, "how much of my ego was tied into being the lawman in the—family."[21] For Martha herself, there is a special kind of honor in doing a job—a job ironically involving guns and violence—that only men have done in the past. "Wearing the uniform of a deputy made her feel—taller. Suddenly she looked like someone that people would pay attention to. For the first time in her life, she felt important. Maybe this is what it feels like to be beautiful, she thought. Only I had to find some other way to achieve it."[22]

There is a great deal of irony in the fact that it is the job of the law to tame the wilderness of those "gallant, romantic, quixotic, courageous" heroes of myth and ballad who fight for honor and individual freedom with guns and violence. As Nora Bonesteel knows, their lives have a significance that must be preserved in the same way that we preserve wilderness, even though to know it intimately is dangerous, perhaps even fatal: "...and she [Nora] would hate to see him [Harm] go, as much as she would hate seeing the last wolf; the last mountain painter [panther]; or even the last timber rattler blotted out of existence. It was a diminishing of sorts."[23]

McCrumb ends her book, appropriately, with a ballad-like epitaph for Harm Sorley, "the last of something." It is offered by Hank the Yank, who takes it from Stephen Vincent Benet's poem about John Brown, a memorable outlaw who gave his life for a law that was higher than the law of his flawed society: "When the last moonshiner buys his radio,/ And the last, lost wild-rabbit of a girl/ Is civilized with a mail-order dress,/ Something will pass that was American/ And all the movies will not bring it back."

But it is precisely the art of McCrumb's book that does bring it back, that shows us "the last of something," that teaches us about a swiftly disappearing way of living and dying. Crafted by a balladeer and an anthropologist, *She Walks These Hills* is at once mystery and tragedy, honoring both the dignity of the outlaw and the necessity of the law. It

---

[21] McCrumb, *Walks*, 331.
[22] McCrumb, *Walks*, 59.
[23] McCrumb, *Walks*, 32.

celebrates the boldness, the admirable outlawry of those who escape from the prison of their ordinary lives and journey homeward, backward, inward, while at the same time it mourns the inescapable tragedy of their deaths. As readers, it is our task to hear the complex chords that are struck in this book. If we read it with a full appreciation for the richness of the artist's art, we will become, like Jeremy, Hank, and Martha, seekers of knowledge, witnesses to the journey, and fellow travelers. Their journey will become our journey, too.

Lot in Life

Names and Places in Sharyn McCrumb's Ballad Series

Scott Crowder-Vaughn

In addition to top-selling works dealing with life in Appalachia, Sharyn McCrumb's Ballad series offers students many oft-missed subtleties. While students might grasp the elements of plot, they are likely to miss the intricacies of how McCrumb seems to appropriately name many of her characters and locales. While the naming of the people and places is certainly not the only means by which students can gain greater insight into the Ballad series, it is certainly a worthwhile study, which can make already student-friendly works even more accessible. Additionally, when certain characters are analyzed in the context of their geographic setting, students discover key insights into the characters' personalities. Throughout the Ballad series, McCrumb closely mingles character's names, locales, and fates in relation to life and death in Wake County. These concepts are to be found in each of the Ballad novels, *If Ever I Return Pretty Peggy-O*, the *Hangman's Beautiful Daughter*, *She Walks These Hills*, the *Rosewood Casket*, and the *Ballad of Frankie Silver*.

In the Ballad series, it all seems to begin with locale. McCrumb begins the first ballad novel, *If Ever I Return Pretty Peggy-O*, with detailed exposition on Sheriff Spencer Arrowood. But Arrowood, by virtue of his position in the community finds his domain in a specific place—the county of his employment, Wake County. McCrumb creates a certain irony when she subtly mentions in passing narrative the name of this county, but for the astute reader, McCrumb is making a sly allusion. With the name "Wake County" McCrumb's readers are alerted to the Appalachian tradition of tending to the dead. A wake is a long funeral ritual during which families and friends keep vigil with their dead. The naming of Wake County is a central element in understanding the Ballad series. For some of the characters, the name of Wake County seems to indicate their fate, acting as a catalyst or harbinger of misfortune or tragedy.

McCrumb expends considerable energy establishing place in the Ballad series. In *If Ever I Return Pretty Peggy-O*, some time is spent contrasting Wake County with its township of Hamelin:

> He took the north road out of town, a street that started as a tree-lined avenue between old white houses sided with fieldstone. At the town limits, the neighborhood dwindled to four-room frame dwellings in need of paint and repair. Then to mobile homes...one mile out, the scene changed to sparse pastures with a few mixed breed Herefords...The road began to rise. It coiled around the mountain so that one side of the highway was a red clay cliff and the other side overlooked a steep slope, thick with trees. Through the leaves of the oaks, one could catch occasional glimpses of the farm and meadows below.[1]

Although Spencer Arrowood proclaims it "beautiful country," subsequent narrative leads readers in another direction: "They got back in the car and headed up the road toward Pigeon Roost, once populated

---

[1] Sharyn McCrumb, *If Ever I Return, Pretty Peggy-O* (New York: Ballantine, 1990) 127–28.

by Grandparents, passenger pigeons, and the ballads of Britain—now a ruin of weathered shanks Kudzu vines, and the last stragglers of the generation before America came to the town."[2]

In sharp contrast to the predictably ordered life of Hamelin, Wake County stands as a dismal (though admittedly more interesting) place indeed. Some of the wording indicates the desolate backwardness found there in a steady progression of dwellings from the nicer to the more impoverished. Even the phrase "mixed breed" used in relation to cows here seems to indicate the true wilderness of Wake County versus homogenous Hamelin.[3] In Hamelin, one is likely to encounter the likes of the humorously named Jessie Traynham, whose last name suggests pleasant luncheons with church friends. In town, the mentally disturbed Vernon Woolwine is a colorful character, but in the county, characters like *Peggy-O's* Roger Gabriel are more menacing.

It is probably no coincidence that city-dwelling police dispatcher turned sheriff's deputy Martha Ayers is one of McCrumb's more self-actualized Ballad series characters. Her name indicates her character, and it gains in significance as Martha becomes more self-actualized and independent. Her name suggests both the biblical Martha and the very air we breathe. By suggesting the biblical character of Martha, we are reminded of devotion, which certainly seems to be the case with Martha Ayers. She is dedicated to her job and to her own self-improvement. Her "air"-like last name indicates the process of her character's development toward transcendence. Though her name initially suggests the fact that she seems ungrounded, her hard work pays off as she earns the job of sheriff's deputy and an education. Though it certainly does not come easy, her transformation remains not in her youth and over the span of five books, Martha is spared the fate of her county counterparts. Martha is allowed to help save lives, while some of her non-city residents seem by mere name and location to be fated for murder or death. In the Ballad series, tragedy strikes in the county, which spawns characters like the ill-fated Harkryder clan, Tammy Robsart, Rita Pentland and the deranged

---

[2] McCrumb, *Peggy-O*, 130.
[3] McCrumb, *Peggy-O*, 127.

Pix-Kyle Weaver. The behaviors and fates of such characters allow Wake County to live up to the implications of its name.

McCrumb often gives Wake County residents names which indicate certain telling aspects of character. In *If Ever I Return Pretty Peggy O*, we meet Pix-Kyle Weaver. Pix-Kyle is from an area of Wake County fittingly called Dark Hollow. Upon reading a name like Pix-Kyle Weaver, the mind stops for a quick second. This is not the sort of name you hear every day, even in the Appalachian region. The name has its connotations that give insight into how McCrumb will develop the character. What are the connotations? As we begin to look closely at the first part of the name, we are reminded of the word "Pixie," which suggests the mischievous. In our first meeting, Pix-Kyle appears as a bit of a pest, foreshadowing his own significance by giving Spencer his "salesman's, 'you haven't heard the last of me' smile."[4] He appears equally annoying when he drops by to visit Deputy Joe LeDonne, attempting to use trickery to get information about Vietnam. Finally, in Peggy Muryan's meeting with Pix-Kyle we are given our strongest indication of Pix-Kyle's mischievous spirit, and mischief seems to be the correct word, for Pix-Kyle seems to believe he is playing a sort of game: "'It was a game, kind of,'" he says. "'Are you going to call my parents?'"[5] But his first name is not the only indicator of Pix-Kyle Weaver's function in the book. Interestingly, Pix-Kyle's last name of Weaver indicates how McCrumb uses him in the story. He is a character whose central personality is not part of the book's action. Literally, however, McCrumb has Pix-Kyle weave in and out of her tale. We are presented with Pix-Kyle in a mere four scenes (not counting the broken up scenes in Peggy Muryan's living room), but like the all-important thread that invisibly holds two seams together, Pix-Kyle is the entity that gives the finished product cohesion. McCrumb has often compared her work to Appalachian quilts; Pix-Kyle is a character who is subtly woven through every square. Pix-Kyle is our first Balled series villain, and as a murderer, a resident of a county whose name anticipates aspects of his character.

---

[4] McCrumb, *Peggy-O*, 25.
[5] McCrumb, *Peggy-O*, 301.

If Pix-Kyle Weaver is a character who enables Wake County to live up to its darkly-charged name, then the Underhill family of *The Hangman's Beautiful Daughter* is a group of characters whose name is inextricably linked to the land, which largely seals their fate. For obvious reasons, the Underhill name is associated with terrain and death, and as the book opens and we discover that they have been murdered in quite a brutal fashion, we realize that we can take the name at its most literal meaning. Again, the brutal character, Josh Underhill (as well as his murdered father), is Pix-Kyle Weaver's neighbor in Dark Hollow. Though the Underhill family is not native to the region, the land seems to determine their fates as well, though that same quality might also benefit a central character later in the book.

The main character is one of the two surviving members of the family, Maggie, who breaks the spell that the land and her very name have over her. Her name is a sort of study in opposites, the bird imagery of the magpie existing in pointed contrast to her earthbound last name. Maggie Underhill is typified as a person trying to overcome the situation of her family, but she is somehow lost. Her abusive family situation, which most Wake County natives never fully grasp, and her previous life elsewhere, Maggie is portrayed as socially and emotionally maladjusted. Like the imitative magpie, she is forced to imitate normalcy. Maggie, as the family's only church-goer, tries to separate herself from her isolationist family, even if she is unconsciously aware of it, so that she can fit in with the area's prevalent religious culture. She also finds a means for escape and imitation through drama, playing the aptly-chosen role of Ophelia with great acumen, as though she felt it "within [her]self"[6] and later to "great applause"[7] before she somehow loses her courage to continue her good work by "mut[ing] her performance to an imitation of the rest of the troupe, intent upon getting her speeches out by rote."[8] Such a statement offers a key insight into Maggie's magpie-like character. Maggie wants out from "under," but she lacks the skills to

---

[6] Sharyn McCrumb, *The Hangman's Beautiful Daughter* (New York: Onyx, 1992) 128.

[7] McCrumb, *Hangman*, 141.

[8] McCrumb, *Hangman*, 141.

achieve it. She mimics to adapt, and therefore survive. So, as has appeared to be her life's pattern, Maggie helps maintain the status quo, even going along with her brother Mark in a quest for an elusive fortune. But Maggie is spared the fate mandated by the land.

As Maggie is saved, one might ponder the question of why. Why is Maggie allowed to live while other characters such as the impoverished Tammy Robsart are fated to die? A possible answer is in the realization of Maggie's status as an outsider. As someone who has lived outside the region, Maggie might be spared in an effort for McCrumb to make a point. A character like Tammy Robsart will not live because of the endemic poverty of her life, born to the region in poverty and dying in much the same fashion, a life with no options and few opportunities, while the non-native Appalachian will ultimately have an easier time remembering and longing for and perhaps achieving a better life because he or she has existed in a more prosperous state. Interestingly, Tammy Robsart dies as the local residents look on, but Maggie is saved, just as though it might seem that the land is about to swallow her, by fellow-outsider, Laura Bruce. As an outsider herself, Laura Bruce, who feels many of the same feelings as Maggie, is able to help Maggie escape her situation, and as Maggie makes it through the baptism-like water, we know that she will have the opportunity for a better life. We know that she has overcome the power of the land and the power of her last name.

The idea of transcendence, though often unachieved, is carried forward in the third book of the Ballad series, *She Walks These Hills*. Once again, the names of the characters are linked to the land and pre-suppose their fate. In this novel, the character Rita Pentland is as doomed as the land of her youthful marriage to Harm Sorley. Rita and Harm are two characters whose names have a meaning beyond their mere syllabic construction. With quite obvious irony, McCrumb gives the escaped prisoner, Harm Sorley his name. Ironically, Harm is quite harmless and has probably always been. He is presented as a character who was quite justified as the killer of a person who raped his land, and now, as a victim of Korsakoff's Syndrome, Harm is hardly (forgiving one skirmish) a menace to society. Harm's property has become the victim of a toxic waste dumping on his small but personally valuable property. He struck out against this injustice in the only way he knew how and killed the person responsible. Still, McCrumb paints a sympathetic portrait of Harm, almost canonizing him through the efforts of a local radio DJ. Perhaps, Harm's name should have been "Harmed" Sorley. But though Harm Sorley has been involved with the land, his name is not associated with the land.

Harm's ex-wife, Rita Pentland, is a character whose name represents her fate mingled with the land. By analyzing her last name in parts, it is easy to make associations with her tragic fate. "Pent" could reference the expression "pent up" which suggests emotion or action unexpressed. This is quite an apt phrase for the character of Rita Pentland. In her new situation with her new husband, Rita first appears to have a comfortable life, but there is evidence that something is missing: "She belonged to the Garden Club..." the text reads.[9] Consequently, "gardening became...something proper to talk about. It didn't matter if you hadn't been to college if you could grow four-foot azalea bushes."[10] Her husband constantly reminds her that she has "come a long way" and that no one could tell that she had once been "white trash."[11] The subtext behind her husband's statements is that Rita has been saved from her previous life with her "murderous" husband. She has been spared the life of Wake county for the hum-drum existence of Hamelin proper. Still, as Rita chooses gardening as a hobby, she shows that she is tied, at least in some small way, to her previous county lifestyle, and as her subsequent actions suggest, Rita is not spared the fate of her name and of the raped portion of Wake County from which she springs. The "land" factor of Rita's name ties directly to the ruined homeplace she can secretly never leave whether through love for her first husband or the subconscious desire to be a part of the land through gardening. As is evident by Rita's actions upon hearing of prior husband Harm's escape, Rita's heart remains with her first husband and their desolate homeplace. But just as Rita cannot fully escape her life in the county, she neither fully escape

---

[9] Sharyn McCrumb, *She Walks These Hills* (New York: Signet, 1994) 39.

[10] McCrumb, *Walks*, 39.

[11] McCrumb, *Walks*, 39.

her new life of "blues and beiges."[12] These two points intersect as her second husband kills her on the contaminated land she so secretly misses.

In two ways, however, Rita and the land receive a sort of vindication as the truth behind the pent up land becomes expressed as the full story is told and in the character of Charlotte, Rita and Harm's daughter. A visit by the EPA is eminent, and her first husband is proven justified as it is discovered why he felt compelled to kill the man who ruined his property and his life. Charlotte, born Chalarty, who has apparently changed her name to better fit with the more cosmopolitan atmosphere at East Tennessee State University, has become a budding geologist, seriously studying the land in a more direct way than Rita's gardening. She is allowed to be what her mother never could. For Rita, such vindications are too late; her life was never fully actualized and, like the land, she remains pent up until the end, a character whose situation ultimately defies transcendence.

McCrumb continues to deal with transcendence in the next Ballad series book, the *Rosewood Casket*. The character of Dovey Stallard relates to the land in a way that threatens to destroy her way of life. Like Maggie Underhill, her name makes for an interesting study of opposites, and her fate, which is still tied to the land, is ambiguous. The bird imagery suggests transcendence, and the last name of Stallard suggests that which is unwilling or unable to move. That is, Dovey Stallard is a character who is both stalled and stalling. While her situation appears apparent, the outcome of her character remains open to interpretation. Dovey Stallard lives up to her name in quite a few ways. Like Rita Pentland, Dovey is not a fully actualized woman; she has given up her life for duty on the farm with her father. She was married, but her husband died, and she seems in search of love with a former suitor whose very essence is his love for the land, but she never achieves more than a platonic friendship. When she reminisces about her childhood, she offers indirect indication that she is aware of the limitations of her life on the farm with her father: "I wanted to be a warrior, not a peacemaker. That's why I picked [Nancy Ward]. You all wanted me to be Rebecca Boone, sweeping the smokehouse while you boys went off to have adventures.

---

[12] McCrumb, *Walks,* 39.

'Be careful, Dan'l.' ...Little girls ought to have somebody to relate to besides pioneer housewives and goody two-shoes Pocahontas."[13]

She appears almost bitterly aware of the demands placed on her life when Clayt Stargill asks her to come and play Nancy Ward in his recreation of the life of Daniel Boone. She sighs as she says no and that "'maybe men don't outgrow play acting, but women do.'"[14] Dovey cannot afford what she perceives to be Clayt's fantasy world of pioneer living. In fact, Clayt, with a name suggesting the clay dirt of the earth, is allowed to have a more healthy relationship with his heritage, the land on which he was conceived. Dovey is grounded in reality and must live with the impending loss of her family farm. She is a character whose life is stalled, but as the plot begins to unfold it is clear that Dovey is attempting to stall the process of losing the land at the hand of real-estate developer Frank Whitescarver, who would literally carve up the land to suit his development strategy.

As Dovey begins to act against her inevitable loss, she starts becoming less stalled and more stalling. She exceeds the role expected of her by becoming a "violent lawbreaker."[15] Deputy Joe LeDonne indicates a popular viewpoint on the expectations of women in his thoughts on Dovey: "Women, in his experience, were not violent lawbreakers, and if they had managed to shoot the boyfriend or otherwise run afoul of the law, they usually stayed put, sobbing as often as not, while they waited to be taken into custody... Women always tried to explain their way our of trouble... She ought to have been waiting for him on the porch, with a box of tissues in her lap, and her lawyer at her elbow."[16]

Dovey's attempt at transcendence, motivated by practicality, has resulted in her attempt to shoot Mr. Whitescarver, which fails as Spencer Arrowood takes the bullet, resulting in his critical injury. Seeking refuge, Dovey makes her way inside the very land that is about to be taken from her, which is ultimately symbolic of her journey inside herself to figure

---

[13] Sharyn McCrumb, *The Rosewood Casket*, (New York: Signet, 1996) 73–74.

[14] McCrumb, *Rosewood*, 75.

[15] McCrumb, *Rosewood, 75*.

[16] McCrumb, *Rosewood,* 316.

out what she needs to do. Deputy LeDonne's confrontation with Dovey in the cave gives the reader final insight into her ambiguous outcome.

Her refusal to leave the land and to die within the cave could be interpreted in different ways. She realizes that if she leaves the cave and surrenders the land, then she will "lose."[17] However, as subsequent narrative indicates, Dovey loses her life, but some evidence exists that in death Dovey achieves the transcendence she truly needs and a literal, permanent connection to the land. A simple statement made by Dovey before she takes her own life tells us that she might have achieved the transcendence her situation would never allow her to otherwise achieve. Taken in context with her first name, Dovey's statement, "All right. I'm coming out" could be interpreted as a statement with larger meaning than a mere diversion for deputy LeDonne.[18] A name like Dovey, which suggests both peace and the possibility of the transcendence of flight, gives insight into how Dovey's suicide can be interpreted. The bird in flight image has been used by writers from Kate Chopin to Bobbie Ann Mason. It is realistic to think that McCrumb would want readers to interpret Dovey's death as one with deep meaning. Importantly, though, Dovey Stallard's fate seems opposite of the similarly named Maggie Underhill. While Maggie's rebirth comes through the water, Dovey meets her fate by falling flat onto the dirt. Dovey's ambiguous outcome makes her among the more interesting protagonists of the Ballad series.

A study of McCrumb's the *Ballad of Frankie Silver*, fittingly leads to a character named Fate. Although neither his name nor his fate is, at first, apparently tied to the land, Fate Harkryder's situation and outcome offer an interesting way to view the larger perspective of names and geographic settings in the Ballad novels. From their first appearance in *She Walks These Hills* to their more fully realized characterizations, the Harkryder clan is typified as one of the most fierce and brutal groups of people in all of the Ballad series. Of course, they hail from the county, this time from a place called Painter Cove, which in *She Walks These Hills* is characterized as a place that "nobody took the road to...unless

---

[17] McCrumb, *Rosewood,* 347.
[18] McCrumb, *Rosewood,* 397.

they were Harkryers or they had to."[19] With their stories of choking poverty and murder, the Harkryders alone could be responsible for how Wake County becomes that which it is called. Their part of the county, Painter Cove, which is derived from the mountain pronunciation of panther with its "curiously human scream"[20] is perhaps most impoverished of all: "They had reached the mouth of Painter Cove, and Martha saw the ramshackle houses and rusting trailers clustered around the dead end of the dirt road. 'Enlightenment appears to be in short supply up here,' she said."[21] In the Ballad series, who is more forlorn than the Harkryders?

Fate Harkryder's first name is designed to make one think of the concept of predestination. Are humans in control of their destiny or are they slaves to predetermined situations and events? Fate Harkryder is a character who is caught in the middle of this struggle. He is in prison for a crime he did not fully commit, but he is on death row as though he were the sole perpetrator. Neither of these aspects fully matter, as former Wake County sheriff Nelse Miller points out because, regardless of his partial innocence or guilt, Fate is a Harkryder: "You could have looked into Fate Harkryder's cradle and tell that he was going to end up in prison. If it wasn't one thing, it'd be another. I've known his kin for more than fifty years, and there's not one solid citizen in the bunch. You'd stand a better chance of getting a thoroughbred out of a swaybacked donkey than you would of getting a good man out of the Harkryder bloodline."[22]

In other words, it is unimportant whether Fate is guilty or not. He is a Harkryder from Painter Cove and by having that name and by being from that place, Fate Harkryder is predetermined by society to be guilty; he is "trash and trouble, like all his kinfolk up there in the holler."[23]

As Fate sits on death row for a crime of which he is only peripherally responsible, it becomes apparent that he will be electrocuted soon. It is out of his hands that he has sat on death row for many years.

---

[19] Sharyn McCrumb, *The Ballad of Frankie Silver* (New York: Signet, 1998) 94.

[20] McCrumb, *Ballad*, 94.

[21] McCrumb, *Ballad*, 101.

[22] McCrumb, *Ballad*, 14.

[23] McCrumb, *Ballad*, 14.

The judge who has granted stays of execution for so long has retired. The parents of the rich victim of the decades old crime are pushing for action, but Spencer Arrowood knows the truth. Fate is being punished for a crime committed largely by his brothers. But after years of unsuccessful appeals, Fate has become resigned to his predestination: "It doesn't matter why I came here," he says, "or whether I deserved it."[24] He insists, "just let it happen."[25] As someone's idea of "trash and trouble," Fate Harkryder's literally fatalistic attitude has been pre-programmed. Through his programmed eyes, Fate Harkryder sees his innocence or guilt as irrelevant. By dying, he lives up to the role that seems to be determined by his very name and his roots in Dark Hollow.

With characters like Martha Ayers, Pix-Kyle Weaver, Maggie Underhill, Rita Pentland, Dovey Stallard and Fate Harkryder, Sharyn McCrumb gives us the material to discuss the many issues surrounding class, education, geographic isolation and the many ways these factors determine one's fate or outcome in life. When students begin to understand these distinctions in the novels, they can begin to see these factors at work in their own personal and regional contexts. While the microcosm known as Wake County is a fictitious town located in the mountain south of Appalachia, the people and their situations—class, isolation and education—are universal. What holds true in Tennessee holds true just as well in Brazil or Mozambique. McCrumb teaches of human potential, of how people can soar or how people can remain enslaved to their lot in life.

---

[24] McCrumb, *Ballad,* 374.
[25] McCrumb, *Ballad,* 375.

A Song to Sing

Women in Sharyn McCrumb's Ballad Series

Nancy K. Jentsch and Danny L. Miller

Though Sharyn McCrumb's acclaimed Ballad Series novels are generally classified as mysteries, they are much broader in scope than simple whodunits. In these novels, McCrumb addresses major themes, such as environmental damage, the loss of land, and injustices in the legal system as they relate to Appalachia. She says: "In my novels I want there to be truth, and an enrichment of the reader's understanding of the mountains and their people."[1] Although Sheriff Spencer Arrowood is the ostensible "main character" and "hero" of the Ballad series, these novels also count among their characters a wide variety of women, who convey another major theme in the novels: the status and roles of women in Appalachian and American society. Many of McCrumb's women characters confront and challenge traditional and stereotypical roles.

Certainly, many of McCrumb's women characters exemplify the traditional roles of women in the Appalachian mountain region, the prescribed roles of homemaker, child rearer, "chief cook and bottle

---

[1] Sharyn McCrumb, "Keepers of the Legends," www.sharynmccrumb.com, 30 April 2003.

washer." This traditional role was described in numerous sociological studies of the early part of the twentieth century. Julian Ralph, for example, in "Our Appalachian Americans" (1903), stated that "mountain women are all drudges after marriage and are married in childhood, [so that] drudging is their lot until they die... They do all the work of cabin and farm... They bear very many children; they cook, wash, mend, weave, knit, plow, hoe, week, milk the cow, and do practically all else that is to be done."[2] Horace Kephart, likewise, in *Our Southern Highlanders* (1913), referring to women's traditional subservient role in the mountain society, stated, "'The woman,' as every wife is called, has her kingdom within the house, and her man seldom meddles with its administration...To [her husband] she is little more than a superior domestic animal."[3] And even as late as the 1960s, Cratis Williams reiterated these views in "The Southern Mountaineer in Fact and Fiction:" "[I]n his family organization the mountain man is the patriarch, the lord of his household. When he gives orders they are obeyed.... There is a traditional division of work in his household. 'There is nothing at which a mountain man or boy balks so positively as doing woman's work. To milk a cow or wash dishes or make a bed is a humiliation not to be borne.' The women do all the work in the home and the garden and assist with the crops."[4]

In all of her Ballad Series novels, McCrumb depicts some women of this type. One example of women in traditional roles in McCrumb's novels is the Stargill womenfolk in *The Rosewood Casket*. Old Randall Stargill's mother, for example, is described as having a "forsythia beauty: a blond brilliance that blooms in earliest spring, lasts only a moment, and then faces, without a trace of its former glory."[5] Lilah Rose Stargill, wife of the eldest brother Robert Lee, refers to the traditional division of roles among men and women when she says to the other women members of the family after they have arrived at the Stargill

---

[2] Ralph Julian, "Our Appalachian Americans," *Harper's New Monthly Magazine* (June 1903): 41.

[3] Horace Kephart, *Our Southern Highlanders* (New York: Outing, 1913) 257.

[4] Cratis Williams, "The Southern Mountaineer in Fact and Fiction, Part I." 3/1 (Autumn 1975): 8–61.

[5] Sharyn McCrumb, *The Rosewood Casket* (New York: Signet, 1996) 148.

homeplace, "This is just like every other family gathering I've ever been to... Men in one room, women in the other." Kelley, the girlfriend of country musician Charles Martin Stargill, replies, "Women in the kitchen...."[6] And the women occupy themselves by making the quilt lining for Randall's coffin, while the menfolks gather in the work shed to make the rosewood casket itself. Tellingly, Frank Whitescarver, the real estate agent out to buy the Stargill property, calls his wife *Squaw*: "This is my territory, Squaw," he tells her, "and I have to keep watch over it."[7]

In McCrumb's depiction of women, there is always an implicit criticism of these traditional roles of men and women, especially in marriage. Marriage seems often—if not always—to be limiting and destructive in McCrumb's novels, reflecting the earlier statements of Ralph, Kephart, and Williams about women's lives of drudgery after marriage. Many of the married women in the Ballad series are depicted as victims of economics and class. In the second of these novels, *The Hangman's Beautiful Daughter*, it seems to an outsider to Wake County that "every woman in Dark Hollow was exactly one man away from welfare."[8] In the third novel, *She Walks These Hills*, Charlotte Sorley compares herself to her mother and says, "I'm getting a master's degree in geology. The first college graduate in the family ever...At least I won't be poor or dependent on some man all my life."[9] Women marry for economic security, like Rita Pentland, in *She Walks These Hills*, or impetuously and impulsively, thinking that their lives will be better, as with Sabrina Harkryder in the same novel. Sabrina marries into the Harkryder clan and "finds herself a captive in the Harkryder's mountain compound. Sabrina kills her baby in order to escape. 'I just had to get away from there... I felt like a prisoner having to stay trapped up there in Painter Cove, missing my own people... I thought if I could just get shut

---

[6] McCrumb, *Rosewood,* 106.

[7] McCrumb, *Rosewood,* 125.

[8] Sharyn McCrumb, *The Hangman's Beautiful Daughter* (New York: Onyx, 1992) 22–23.

[9] Sharyn McCrumb, *She Walks These Hills* (New York: Scribners, 1994) 220.

of this kid, things could go back to being like they was before, and I'd be free to leave.'"[10]

In *She Walks These Hills*, Harm Sorley's ex-wife Rita "leaves the respectability of her prison-like second marriage ('spending her life being grateful and walking a social chalkline') to search for Harm. Upon her return to their abandoned trailer home, she is murdered by her second husband [Euell Pentland], enraged at her unfaithfulness."[11] Euell speaks condescendingly of Rita: she "could be thoughtless at times," he says, "Her class doesn't observe the social niceties."[12] He believes and makes her believe that he has saved her from something awful: "She'd come a long way, Euell liked to say. With her beauty parlor-styled hair, and her dresses of blues and beiges from Montaldos, and their carefully furnished house, couldn't nobody tell she'd started out as white trash. He'd saved here from that, and she knew it."[13] Rita's leaving of Euell Pentland to try to find and rejoin Harm is a kind of emancipation for her from the strictures of "respectability" she has had to endure as Euell's wife.

There is a similar message about marriage in *The Ballad of Frankie Silver*. A lowland woman, Miss Mary Erwin, sister-in-law of Burgess Gaither, the clerk of the Superior Court of Burke County, North Carolina, who is the narrator of the Frankie Silver portion of the novel, is unmarried. Miss Mary goes to court to see the trial of Frankie Silver, although women were not usually permitted and certainly not thought respectable for attending, thus challenging the conventions of her day. She is often compared in the novel to her more demure and traditional sister, Burgess Gaither's wife Elizabeth. When Frankie Silver "confesses" that she killed her husband Charlie because he was a brute who threatened to kill her and their infant daughter Nancy, Miss Mary's response to Burgess is telling: "'People wonder why I never married... There is too much risk in the venture. A woman is quite at the mercy of a

---

[10] Susan Wittig Albert, "The Art of Sharyn McCrumb, Anthropologist and Balladeer" Sharyn McCrumb Press Kit, 7.

[11] Albert, "Art," 7.

[12] McCrumb, *Walks*, 218.

[13] McCrumb, *Walks,* 24.

fool or a brute, and one can never know the bargain one has made until it is too late.'"[14]

Certainly, Miss Mary's words are borne out in the story of Frankie Silver and her husband Charlie. In her testimony concerning Frankie Silver, her half-sister-in-law Margaret Silver reveals much about Frankie's life:

> She's [Frankie's] just two years older than me, but prettier—I'll give her that... The truth is sometimes I wished I was more like her. She was little and fair, and she worked hard, too. Of course, she had to. Being married to Charlie and all... About Frankie. Well, she kept that cabin clean, saw to the baby, tended the cows and the chickens, and did the cooking and the washing and kept the fire going. There are three of us girls to help Mama do what Frankie did all by herself. That set me against marrying up early, too."[15]

Frankie is a woman trapped in a traditional mountain marriage, and she holds the reader's (and McCrumb's) sympathy throughout the novel.

Comments about marriage such as Miss Mary's above and depictions of brutish marriages like that of Charlie and Frankie Silver suggest McCrumb's feelings about the traditional roles of women, especially in marriage. Perhaps her attitude is summed up in the title of one of her Elizabeth McPherson novels, *If I'd Killed Him When I Met Him*. This latter novel prompted Charles Silet in an interview in the *Armchair Detective* to ask McCrumb, "What would you say to somebody who said, 'Gee, you really seem down on men?'" McCrumb doesn't explicitly answer the question, but it is apparent in her response that she feels that women have been victimized by men throughout history, and that they must now end that victimization and find emancipation from the traditional roles of women. McCrumb replied, "I was anticipating that question when they sent me out on tour." She then discusses a song popularized by the Kingston Trio entitled "Delia's Gone" which

---

[14] Sharyn McCrumb, *The Ballad of Frankie Silver* (New York: Dutton, 1998) 275.

[15] McCrumb, *Ballad*, 82.

"sounded in their version like guy's girlfriend had left him." But when she heard Johnny Cash's version, she says, the song sounded as if the man had killed Delia. Men killing their sweethearts or wives "has been in the canon for centuries," says McCrumb. Certainly, a great many of the Scottish, English, and Appalachian ballads, with which McCrumb is very familiar, are murder ballads in which innocent women are killed by their lovers. "Almost every folk song—'The Banks of the Ohio'—are all about murdered women," says McCrumb. "I just thought it was time somebody shot back."[16] McCrumb thinks it is time women stood up for themselves; even when the results are sometimes tragic—at least women are not passive victims. And, in fact, many of the women in the Ballad series do "shoot back." Dovey Stallard shoots at (but misses) Frank Whitescarver, the land-hungry real estate agent in *The Rosewood Casket,* and she dies upholding her belief in the injustice of a government that would allow her family's farm to be lost; Peggy Muryan shoots her would-be rapist and murderer in *If Ever I Return, Pretty Peggy-O;* and Frankie Silver kills her husband with an ax in *The Ballad of Frankie Silver.*

Very often, McCrumb describes the married woman in these novels as seemingly lifeless, using adjectives such as "beige" and "oatmeal" to describe them, their dull lives, their clothing, and their home décor. Rita Pentland, for example, when thinking about the flowers in her garden, muses, "You didn't have to be careful with them like you did with clothes. It was all right not to have beige ones."[17] Besides the beige and blue clothes that Euell has provided to show her "respectability," Rita has a beige sofa,[18] beige carpeting,[19] and a respectable tan coat.[20] Her bedroom is described as being "as colorless as the rest of Rita Pentland's house."[21] Beige is a bland color, symbolic of dullness, lifelessness, and aridity.

---

[16] Charles Silet, "She Walks These Hills: An Interview with Sharyn McCrumb" *The Armchair Detective* 28/4 (Fall 1995): 373.
[17] McCrumb, *Walks*, 24.
[18] McCrumb, *Walks*, 217.
[19] McCrumb, *Walks*, 219.
[20] McCrumb, *Walks*, 220.
[21] McCrumb, *Walks*, 219.

In contrast to these "beige" women, trapped in marriages, which prevent them from having their own identities, several of McCrumb's women characters challenge the traditional and stereotypical roles of mountain women. In the *Rosewood Casket*, for example, in contrast to the Stargill womenfolks noted above, we have the character of Dovey Stallard, who at the end of the novel tragically dies defending her family's land. Dovey is still unmarried at age thirty-five (actually she is secretly the widow of Dwayne Stargill, the wild reckless Stargill who was the only one who could make her laugh and who died in a car wreck before his new bride Dovey could join him in Florida, but for all intents and purposes she has been unmarried.) Throughout the novel, Dovey is described as a competent, "take-charge" person, and the fact that she becomes a "warrior" defending her land is foreshadowed in her childhood when she plays pioneers with the Stargill boys. When they want Dovey to play a traditional woman to their white men pioneers, Dovey chooses instead to play Nancy Ward, a Cherokee woman Indian chief.

When Clayt Stargill reminds Dovey of this game in later years, he says that she tricked them by not telling them the whole truth about Nancy Ward, that she had later become a peacemaker who protected the whites from the wrath of the Cherokees. Dovey says, "Of course I didn't...I wanted to be a warrior, not a peacemaker. That's why I picked her. You all wanted me to be Rebecca Boone, sweeping the smokehouse while you boys went off to have adventures."[22] Dovey is glad Clayt sometimes tells the students for whom he does reenactments of Daniel Boone about Nancy Ward. "Good," she says, "Little girls ought to have somebody to relate to besides pioneer housewives and goody-two-shoes Pocohantas... I hope you make it clear that women played an important role in Cherokee society and that [Nancy Ward] had real power and influence."[23] Later, when Dovey is on the run after she has shot Spencer Arrowood (she intended to shoot Frank Whitescarver), she explains to young Kayla Johnson, whom she has kidnapped: "The Stargill boys and I used to pretend we were pioneers. They were always Daniel Boone,

---

[22] McCrumb, *Rosewood*, 73–74.
[23] McCrumb, *Rosewood*, 74.

Davy Crockett, and John Sevier... Clayt always wanted me to be Daniel's wife. I had to go down to the library to find somebody more fun than old Rebecca Boone, who mostly stayed home raising babies. I decided to be a Cherokee chief named Nancy Ward."[24] Dovey concedes to Kayla that Nancy was "friendly to the whites," but "she could fight when she had to. Once when the Cherokees were at war with the Creeks, Nancy Ward won the battle. She picked up her dead husband's rifle and led the charge against the enemy."[25]

When her father seems to resign himself to the sale of the land ("Maybe the Lord wants us to quit the land, and find another life,") Dovey reacts:

> I don't want another life," said Dovey. 'I can go out and get a job. You know I wouldn't mind doing it if we need the money. I could get on the night shift somewhere—a factory, maybe— and still do my work around here in the daytime. I should have done that when we lost the barn, but you were too stubborn to let me. I don't know why I let you talk me out of it then.' 'Your mother never worked, Dovey.' She sighed. 'That was a long time ago, Daddy. Different world. Besides, Mama had a husband and two kids to raise, and her share of the Farm to run. Nobody worked harder than Mama did...[26]

Dovey erupts when her father suggests they wait for the Lord to grant them a miracle: "Oh, crap, Daddy! Faith isn't going to get those tax wolves off our doorstep. We have to fight to keep what's ours."[27]

Besides women like Dovey, two of the Ballad series' major recurring female characters, Nora Bonesteel and Martha Ayers, are explicit foils to the traditional stereotype. Different in many ways, surely, both Nora and Martha are women who have learned or are learning to stand on their own. While in some ways reflecting the traditional roles of

---

[24] McCrumb, *Rosewood,* 365.
[25] McCrumb, *Rosewood,* 356.
[26] McCrumb, *Rosewood,* 220.
[27] McCrumb, *Rosewood,* 220.

women in Appalachian (and general) society (society hasn't completely changed, after all), both Nora and Martha challenge those roles. Nora is a strong, competent, fulfilled mountain woman of the older generation, while Martha is an example of the post-feminist emancipated woman searching for her identity.

Nora Bonesteel could be said to fit into a long line of Appalachian "granny women" or "witches" (such as Mary Dorthula White in Mildred Haun's the *Hawk's Done Gone*, Granny Younger in Lee Smith's *Oral History* or Aunt Granny Lith in Chris Offutt's story of that title). Although she could easily be a stereotype, however, she emerges from the Ballad series not as a curiosity or an eccentric, but as a well-rounded and sympathetic character, not perceived as weird or strange. In fact, she is a well-respected member of her community. All that really seems to differentiate her from her neighbors is her ability to see things that will happen or to see the ghosts of the dead, the Sight, inherited from her Celtic forebears (her grandmother Flossie also had the Sight). Nora is perhaps one of the favorite characters among readers of McCrumb's novels.

One description of Nora occurs in the Prologue to the *Hangman's Beautiful Daughter*:

> She was well past seventy, and she lived alone in a white frame house up on the part of Ashe Mountain that had been Bonesteel land since 1793... She seldom left her mountain fastness except to walk down the gravel road to church on Sunday morning, but she had a goodly number of visitors—mostly people wanting advice... Folks said that no matter how early you reached her house of a morning with a piece of bad news, she'd meet you on the porch with a mug of fresh brewed chicory coffee, already knowing what it was you'd come about. Nora Bonesteel did not gossip. The telephone company had never got around to stringing the lines up Ashe Mountain. She just knew. Dark Hollow folk, most of them kin to her, anyhow, took it for granted, but it made some of the townspeople down in Hamelin afraid... Nobody in Dark Hollow ever mistook her for a witch. She taught Sunday school to the

early teens, and she kept her place in an old King James Bible with the feather of a red-bird's wing. Nora Bonesteel never wished harm, never tried to profit by her knowledge....And if she did impart a warning, she'd look away while she told it, and say what she had to say in a sorrowful way that was nobody's idea of a curse...[28]

Throughout the Series, Nora's gift of the Sight is a given, and it is clear that she is not a witch.

McCrumb does indeed state that some people are "afraid" of Nora Bonesteel, but she is careful to show that many others are not and do not see her as unusual or frightening. She has many friends. She is Spencer Arrowood's good friend, for example, as she is a friend to Laura Bruce in the *Hangman's Beautiful Daughter*. Laura often comes to see Nora in times of trouble, to be comforted by her (instead of going to visit the Underhill children whose parents have been murdered, Laura turned off "before she reached their road, and headed up Ashe Mountain to spend a comforting morning with Nora Bonesteel."[29]) And it is to Nora that Spencer's mother Jane Arrowood often turns for companionship and comfort. When Spencer is shot, Jane seeks Nora for comfort. In fact, Jane Arrowood is in many ways throughout the novels a foil for Nora. Jane has devoted her life to a husband and children; Nora is unmarried and has in effect devoted her life to the community.

Nora is not only a good friend, she is also the repository of much mountain folklore and legend. In *She Walks These Hills*, Nora is described:

> While the mortal remains of Geneva Albright were being consigned to the earth of Oakdale Cemetery, Nora Bonesteel kept her vigil alone in her friend's tiny cottage. They had been friends for sixty years and more, sharing a girlhood of church picnics and square dances in Dark Hollow, and losing touch at maturity...Nora saw her old friend from one year to the next...

---

[28] McCrumb, *Hangman,* 11–14.
[29] McCrumb, *Hangman,* 75.

She had held the new babies, wrapped in the fleecy woolens knitted for them by "Aunt" Nora...[30]

While Geneva's children are attending the funeral, Nora Bonesteel goes through the old mountain rituals in honor of her friend: she puts away the honey because you don't eat honey on the day of a funeral; she stops all the clocks; she opens all the doors and windows; she goes out to inform the bees in their hives of Geneva's death and ties a black ribbon on the lid of the bee hive.

These actions show not only Nora's affection for and life-long friendship with Geneva, but her extensive knowledge of much of the ancient lore of the mountains, something that McCrumb obviously thinks is very important—the old ways which have mostly been forgotten. Nora is a "keeper of the legends." For example, it is Nora who knows what a Scripture cake is in *The Rosewood Casket.* As Nora thinks about Harm Sorley in *She Walks These Hills* she muses: "It was a sad thing about Harm Sorley, dangerous as he might be. He was still the last of something, and she would hate to see him go, as much as she would hate to see the last wolf, the last mountain painter, or even the last timber rattler out of existence. It was a diminishing of sorts."[31] As the mountain lore, rituals and parts of nature fade, Nora maintains a sympathetic link with them.

Nora is described throughout the novels as a competent, strong woman, at peace with herself. When Laura Bruce comes to see her in *The Hangman's Beautiful Daughter*, Nora is described: "Even at her age, her lean body looked wiry rather than frail...."[32] She "never asked favors of a soul."[33] Nora also finds peace in and with nature. She has removed the wall from one side of her house and has a floor to ceiling picture window so she can look on the mountain vista. She regrets (as another "diminishing" of things) the loss of the chestnut trees to the blight, which destroyed them. She has a pet groundhog named Persey (Persephone).

---

[30] McCrumb, *Walks,* 101.
[31] McCrumb, *Walks,* 18.
[32] McCrumb, *Hangman,* 28.
[33] McCrumb, *Ballad,* 19.

Nora is, in fact, a complex, many-faceted woman. She is full of pithy sayings. She weaves and knits. She has a good sense of humor (often telling jokes which others don't readily get). She listens to classical music. She has read and can quote Thomas Wolfe. She watches soap operas. Her house is "cozy" and comfortable.[34] Preserving tradition, she brings the scripture cake to Randall Stargill's funeral. She is at peace with herself as few people are. Nora is also certainly a non-traditional woman in many ways (while ironically maintaining many of the fast-disappearing Appalachian traditions)—she lives alone with nature as her chief companion, and she takes care of herself—and others.

Significantly, Nora Bonesteel has never married:

> She had never married. Occasionally, a teenager in calf love would ask her why, as if she'd missed out on the most marvelous experience imaginable, and she had a string of quick answers to reel off. I didn't know the last man to ask me would be the last man to ask me. My sweetheart was killed at Chickamauga. (She didn't use that one much these days. Young people had no sense of history of missed the joke.) I put the last stitch in a Lone Star quilt and doomed myself to spinsterhood. The real reasons were more complex. She was an only child who had learned early to live with solitude, and finally, to like it. Her mother's illness kept her tied down for most of her twenties, and then she had inherited the house, so there was no great need to wed just for the sake of stability. She made a little money with her needlework, her goats, and her garden crops, but on a rural farm a little money was quite enough. So the urgency was lacking.[35]

Emancipated from the traditional reasons for marriage, Nora has been free to become herself, the person she is.

Martha Ayers in the Ballad series is also by no means a stereotypical mountain woman. She is a child of the 1960s and of the many changes, including in male-female relationships, which began to

---

[34] McCrumb, *Walks*, 118.
[35] McCrumb, *Hangman*, 107–108.

occur in the entire country, and is someone with whom many women can identify. Martha becomes in the novels an exemplum of the post-feminist emancipated woman. Although she seems at first to have tried to find her identity in men or to need a relationship with one to be fulfilled, Martha comes to find her own identity in many other aspects of her life. Martha is certainly a person in search of herself. She develops throughout the course of the novels from a somewhat shallow and even unlikable woman with a low self-esteem to a person comfortable with herself, showing courage, determination and strength. Martha eventually begins to attain the two things she most desires for her life: a loving relationship with a man and a fulfilling career.

When we first meet Martha in *If Ever I Return, Pretty Peggy-O*, she is working as a dispatcher in Spencer Arrowood's office. She has been married and divorced twice; as McCrumb puts it, she is between husbands. At this point in her life, Martha seems to have little confidence in herself and a low self-esteem. One of the subplots of this novel involves the preparations being made for the twentieth reunion of Hamelin High School's class of 1966. Martha heads up the reunion committee and is assisted by two former classmates, Tyndall Johnson Garner and Sally Howell. Not only were these women popular in high school, but they have each attained part of what Martha sseks: Tyndall is married with a family, and Sally has a Ph.D. and a career. Martha's words are: "One of them is a professor, and the other one is married. I guess they both have me beat. Always did, always will."[36]

Martha is obviously still uncomfortable with herself in comparison to these two women, just as she was in high school. In discussing plans for the reunion and the possible appearance there of Peggy Muryan, the famous folk singer, McCrumb writes, "Martha smiled brightly. 'Maybe we could play her old record album and she could lip sync!' As soon as she said it, she could tell from their [Tyndall's and Sally's] expressions that she had said something uncool—gauche—not with it. After all these years, it still hurt."[37] Despite the lingering hurt, however, Martha still

---

[36] Sharyn McCrumb, *If Ever I Return, Pretty Peggy-O* (New York: Ballantine, 1990) 149.

[37] McCrumb, *Peggy-O*, 145.

continues to idolize these women, reverting to behavior more typical of a high schooler than a thirty-eight year old woman: Tyndall and Sally weren't the 'popular girls in class' anymore, but Martha couldn't get over the feeling of intimidation. Well, not intimidation really. Just being over impressed—she had a crazy urge to tell somebody about their visit: you know, casually, 'Oh Tyndall Johnson Garner and Dr. Sally Howell dropped by my place for dinner last night.' As if they were royalty. She hoped her feelings didn't show."[38]

McCrumb adds an interesting twist to our view of Martha's self-image, however, in a thought of Tyndall's in the next chapter of the book: "Martha would know [about the murder in town], since she worked at the sheriff's office. Tyndall sighed. Martha had such an interesting life."[39] Even at this early point in McCrumb's depiction of Martha, she makes it clear that Martha's life may appear more exciting and fulfilled to others than to herself, and may actually be more exciting than she knows.

In the later novels, Martha moves up from being a dispatcher to become a deputy sheriff herself, and she learns to value herself as a person, as others also learn to respect her. At the end of *The Hangman's Beautiful Daughter* as Martha takes charge of the flood rescue operations, Spencer Arrowood tells her, "You've done a good job."[40] Susan Wittig Albert summarizes: "Martha Ayers [in *She Walks These Hills*] is a newly-appointed deputy who plans to capture Harm [Sorley] as 'her ticket to a permanent deputy' and to earn the respect of her lover, Deputy Joe LeDonne. Martha's search...is an initiation into the mystery of her own nature and into her relationship with her lover, as well as her profession as a law officer."[41] As a result of becoming a deputy sheriff, Martha must confront some of her culture's attitudes about masculinity. Speaking of "the ambiguous motif of honor" in *She Walks These Hills* (particularly masculine honor involving war and violence), which she says "underlies much of the book," Albert asserts: "Honor is almost

---

[38] McCrumb, *Peggy-O*, 132–33.
[39] McCrumb, *Peggy-O*, 155.
[40] Albert, "Art," 12.
[41] Albert, "Art," 12.

always coupled with a kind of hyper-masculinity ('macho games,' the sheriff calls it) and with violence. As a woman and a law officer, Martha sees the danger in a culture where honor and guns breed death."[42] Martha's "insight into the ambiguity of honor," says Albert, is ironic because, "For Martha herself, there is a special kind of honor in doing a job—a job ironically involving guns and violence—that only men have done in the past."[43] Martha's insight helps to show that she is a complex person trying to come to terms with the roles of men and women in modern society.

Martha's goals of a loving relationship and a fulfilling career become intertwined in *She Walks These Hills*. The theme of life as a journey is quite strong in this novel, and the book is crucial in the story of Martha's journey to self-acceptance. In the course of this novel, she practically demands that Spencer Arrowood make her a deputy, which gives her a new sense of personal worth. McCrumb writes of Martha: "Wearing the uniform of a deputy made her feel—taller. Suddenly she looked like someone that people would pay attention to. For the first time in her life, she felt important. Maybe this is what it feels like to be beautiful, she thought. Only I had to find some other way to achieve it."[44] Of her decision to become a deputy, Martha says to Joe in her thoughts: "I try to better myself so you'll be proud of me."[45] Later in the novel, she confronts him with these words: "I was working sixteen-hour days, trying to become something more than a jumped-up secretary. Trying to be someone whose judgment you could respect."[46]

In her attempts to improve her standing with Joe, however, she actually makes him "edgy," which prompts him to avoid her.[47] Eventually, he strays. Faced with this crisis in their relationship, Martha shows how much she counts on Joe and their relationship in these words: "Because if I hate him, I'm left with nothing."[48] Despite her new career,

---

[42] McCrumb, *Walks*, 7–8.

[43] Albert, "Art," 12.

[44] McCrumb, *Walks*, 59.

[45] McCrumb, *Walks*, 201.

[46] McCrumb, *Walks*, 332.

[47] McCrumb, *Walks*, 128.

[48] McCrumb, *Walks*, 229.

Martha feels she would be lost—would have, and perhaps be, nothing without Joe. At this point in their relationship, it may seem as if Martha is anything but a post-feminist emancipated woman, for she seems to be doing things to make herself better only to please a man, receive praise and respect from him, rather than for herself, but later Martha places her relationship with Joe in another perspective. At the end of *She Walks These Hills*, after Joe has had an affair with Crystal Stanley, the waitress at the Mockingbird Inn, he apologizes to Martha. Martha says to Joe, "You're going to have to get better at [talking about things], because I'm not going to be shut out again while you indulge your own pain. You treat me as a friend first, a woman second. Got that? I may not have a penis, LeDonne, but I sure as hell have a gun."[49] Martha learns to respect herself and expects the same from Joe:

> Regarding Martha's growth in the Ballad Series, McCrumb herself says, 'She evolved.' I was probably, in the first chapter of *Peggy-O*, not terribly kind to her. She's the one who suggested that for the drunk-driving speech, Spencer read, 'Please God, I'm Only Seventeen' from Ann Landers. But she grew through that book, and she's not a woman that I would normally identify with. She didn't go to college; she's not intellectual; she wouldn't know Marlowe from Morgan Fairchild, so she's not somebody that I would put my ego in. But I grew to respect her by the end of the book. I really thought she was a very sensible and a very strong woman.[50]

McCrumb continues to show Martha's personal growth and to create respect and admiration for her in the later novels in the series. Many readers obviously find this kind of character appealing. They can identify with Martha's struggles to overcome women's society-imposed limitations and find self-respect and personal fulfillment—the post-feminist woman's great challenge.

---

[49] McCrumb, *Walks,* 332.
[50] Silet, "Interview," 378.

Certainly since the 1960s and the feminist movement, women have struggled between the roles of wife and mother or career. Says Kathleen Maio:

> Not surprisingly, perhaps, some of [McCrumb's] most insightful scenes [in *If Ever I Return, Pretty Peggy-O*] have little to do with her mystery plot… The segment of the class of 1966 that McCrumb knows well, and that she explores for the reader with some sensitivity, is the women. The girls who came of age in the mid-1960s are now women trapped between Jane Wyatt domesticity and career-oriented superwomanhood. Finding both extremes equally unappealing, were never sure what they were supposed to make of their lives. And now, looking back, they're at a loss as to how to measure their successes and failures.[51]

Discussing the dilemma confronting the 1960s (and post-1960s) woman in the *Armchair Detective* interview, McCrumb says: Choice A is to get married and have children; Choice B is "to do the whole career thing and try to have it all and stretch yourself out and then no matter what happens to your kid, if he gets a D in Spanish, it's your fault because you weren't home playing Sesame Street flash cards with him. So that was two wrong answers."[52] Referring to Tyndall and Sally in *If Ever I Return, Pretty-O*, by who Martha has been intimidated and whom she has idolized for their "successes" in marriage and career, McCrumb says, "So Tyndall and Sally were two wrong answers for women [in the 1960s]."[53] For Martha Ayers the struggle is to find the "right" answer—a combination of both a fulfilling male/female relationship and a job/career. Significantly, Martha and Joe have yet to marry in the series.

Many of McCrumb's characters have theme songs. She says, "Every one of my characters has a theme song…Spencer Arrowood's is a Don Williams song called 'Good Ol' Boys Like Me'" (an ironic theme

---

[51] Kathleen Maio, "Murder in Print," *Wilson Library Bulletin* (September 1990): 106.

[52] Silet, "Interview," 377.

[53] Silet, "Interview," 378.

song).[54] Harm Sorley's is "Fox on the Run." We have tried to think of what theme songs McCrumb might give to Nora Bonesteel and Martha Ayers. Nora's would almost have to be a hymn or a ballad, something combining both her Christian beliefs of kindness and goodness and her natural/supernatural insights. Martha's might be "I Am Woman," the anthem of the women's movement of the 1960s, or "I'm a W-O-M-A-N."

---

[54] Silet, "Interview," 377.

Mythical Mountains

The Mythology of

Sharyn McCrumb's Ballad Series

Kimberley M. Holloway

Sharyn McCrumb, like many who write about the Appalachian mountains and the people who inhabit them, weaves the mythology of her Celtic background into the stories she creates. In the Ballad series, especially, themes and stories from Celtic mythology are the backdrop against which she works her magic. McCrumb's Ballad series, which consists of *If Ever I Return, Pretty Peggy-O, The Hangman's Beautiful Daughter, She Walks These Hills, The Rosewood Casket, The Ballad of Frankie* Silver, and *The Songcatcher* contains such Celtic themes as the cycle of nature; the significance of boundaries, borders, and water; the triple goddess; and the second sight. These mythological themes, found throughout the series, give it a sense of purpose and direction.

Especially important in these novels is McCrumb's use of the cycle of nature and the observations of the Celtic Ritual calendar. Rebecca L. Briley writes that "the people of the region [Appalachia] experience a oneness with nature and the land itself, but the cyclical pattern of the eternal return in nature is an integral part of their religious beliefs and their outlook in life."[1] As with the ancient Celts, the cycle of nature is an important aspect in the lives of the inhabitants of McCrumb's fictional Hamelin, Tennessee, and the events of these novels mirror the cycles of the Celtic Ritual Calendar.

Under Druid leadership, the ancient Celtic Ritual calendar was originally based on a three-year system of celebrating four great festivals. These festivals were held exactly nine months apart and resulted in a complete cycle of festivals every thirty-six months or three years. In addition, their system of alternating "good" and "bad" months coincided with new and old moon cycles.[2]

When the Romans introduced their lunar and solar thinking to the Celts, this three-year cycle was replaced by a new Celtic Ritual calendar. In this new calendar, all four great festivals were observed every year rather than every three years. The beginning of the Celtic ritual year began on 1 November with Samhain, one of the two most significant festivals celebrated by the Celts. This festival was a time of remembering the dead, whom the Celts believed roamed the earth on this day bordering the old and new years. On 1 February, the Celts celebrated Imbolc. The purpose of this festival was to "encourage fertility and the emergence of the sun from its winter sleep."[3] Held to honor St. Brigid, a Celtic fertility goddess, it was a time of weddings and renewed fertility for humans, animals, and the earth. Beltane, the second of the Celts' important festivals, was held on 1 May and celebrated the beginning of summer. The two important festivals of Samhain and Beltane, marking the beginning of winter and summer, were considered times of increased spiritual activity. Finally, Lughnasadh, held on 1 August, was a summer festival marking the end of summer and the beginning of harvest.

McCrumb uses these festival times to carry her characters and stories through the cycle of life. *If Ever I Return, Pretty Peggy-O* takes place during the time of Midsummer and Lughnasadh, festivals important to the agricultural Celts. In this novel, McCrumb uses both

---

[1] Rebecca L. Briley, "River of Earth: Mythic Consciousness in the Works of James Still" *Appalachian Heritage* 9/2 (1981): 53.

[2] John Sharkey, *Celtic Mysteries: Ancient Tradition in Ireland and Wales* (London: Thames and London, 1975) 17.

[3] Sharkey, *Mysteries*, 18.

ritual animal and human sacrifice to illustrate the mythological importance of this time of year. Obsessed with reenacting scenes from Vietnam and getting the attention of a folksinger, a young man ritually kills a dog, a sheep, and, finally, a young, unmarried girl.

In the last three novels in the Ballad series, McCrumb explores the Celtic Ritual calendar in more depth. the *Hangman's Beautiful Daughter*, which takes place in winter, most vividly illustrates this calendar. Beginning at Samhain, McCrumb guides her characters through the winter to Beltane and the beginning of spring. Ritual sacrifice is an essential element of this season in which the Celts worshipped their sun god. Both fire and water receive sacrifices before the novel concludes: A young mother dies in a trailer fire, and the river, in which Celts traditionally offered sacrifices, overflows taking both possessions and human life with it.

In the *Hangman's Beautiful Daughter*, the epigraph for the prologue is "Summer for the living, Winter for the dead—The Rule for Solstice Alignment for Standing Stones in Pre-Christian Britain."[4] In the novel, McCrumb writes, "The cycle of seasons had been going on a long time for the mountain people. Not just in the Appalachians, with the descendants of Germans, Scots, Irish, Welshmen, and all the other settlers, but long before that, when an ancient tribe, the Celtic hearth culture in Switzerland had observed the changing year with similar customs."[5]

This novel opens at the time of Samhain, the beginning of winter for the Celts. Samhain began a time of death in nature and, for the characters in the novel, death is the defining feature of this season. Five members of one family, a young mother, and an old man all face death during this time in nature's cycle. *The Hangman's Beautiful Daughter* ends in April, just before Beltane, the spring festival—a time of renewal and rebirth. Though death has reigned during the winter months, healing begins with the coming of spring. Laura Bruce, though her baby is born dead, becomes a mother as a result of another young mother's death. Spring

---

[4] Sharyn McCrumb, *The Hangman's Beautiful Daughter* (New York: Onyx, 1992) 11.

[5] McCrumb, *Hangman*, 188–89.

brings a new life to the Bruce family as well as a renewal of life to the community.

In *She Walks These Hills*, McCrumb uses the time of Lughnasadh—the beginning of autumn—to illustrate that summer is over in nature as well as in the lives of some of the characters. The autumn season in Wake County is a time of ritual sacrifice as well. Both child and animal sacrifices play a secondary role in the events of this novel. The story of the elephant that was executed for murder in east Tennessee and a young mother's desperate attempt to gain freedom by killing her baby characterizes this season in Wake County. The novel culminates in an old man's death by fire, a quite effective illustration of the ritual burnt offering.

The cycles of nature are also evident in *The Rosewood Casket*, where a man is dying just as the rest of the world is preparing to enter spring—the time of renewal. Spring Equinox is sometimes called the Festival of Trees, and trees play an important role in this novel.[6] A man saves a precious supply of rosewood and asks his sons to build his casket with it. Ritual burial sacrifice is also illustrated in this novel. When Dovey Stallard, a fugitive from the law, hides in a cave, it becomes a place of death. In order to save her honor, and maybe even her land, Dovey goes into the earth and does not return alive.

Equally important is McCrumb's use of the mountains as borders or boundaries. Borders in Celtic myth are mystical, supernatural places where anything can happen. Celts placed great importance on "the dwelling place of the beings of the other-world."[7] This dwelling place, called the Sidh, is an in-between place—a border—of extraordinary supernatural power. As a result of this belief, the Celts placed great emphasis on the idea of borders—physical, spiritual, or temporal—and considered them places or times in which the potential for signs, omens, or other portents of the future was possible. Other in-between states or borders included twilight—the border between day and night;

---

[6] Isaac Bonewits, "A Neopagan Druid Calendar," http://www.qed.net/bonewits/NeodruidismCalendar.HTML, April 1997.

[7] Sharkey, *Mysteries*, 6.

dew—water which does not come from sea, rain, rivers, or wells; and mistletoe—neither a plant nor a tree.[8]

The Celts believed that the lines dividing time periods such as days, years, or seasons were "haunted by a mysterious power which has a propensity both for good and for evil."[9] Sunrise and sunset were considered dangerous times to be outside: Both "midday and midnight, like sunrise and sunset, were moments when the veil between this world and the unseen world was very thin."[10]

Samhain and Beltane, which divide the two halves of the year—summer and winter—were considered especially potent boundaries. Other important times of division were Imbolc or St. Brigid's night—the eve of 1 February—which divided the winter half of the year into winter and spring and Lughnasadh—August—which divided the summer half of the year into summer and autumn. The three times of year considered most spiritually potent were the border times of May Eve, November Eve, and Midsummer's Eve. These times were called "spirit nights," and supernatural power abounded then.[11]

Whereas in many cultures the New Year has long been considered a time of new beginnings and order in life, the Celtic New Year began a time of "the elimination of boundaries between the dead and the living, between the sexes, between one man's property and another's and, in divinations, between the present and the future...the return of chaos."[12] Samhain, the border between the new year and the old, was considered the most spiritually active time of year. Today, Halloween retains much of the mystery and supernatural quality of the Celtic belief in the importance of this border time.

Though Summer's Eve and May Eve do not contain the negative characteristics of Samhain, they were still observed as important border times. While a person's fortune may have hung in the balance on the border between the first half of summer and the last half, "one is not

---

[8] Sharkey, *Mysteries,* 11.
[9] Alwyn Rees and Brinley Rees, *Celtic Heritage: Ancient Tradition in Ireland and Wales* (London: Thames and Hudson, 1961) 9.
[10] Rees, *Heritage,* 91.
[11] Rees, *Heritage,* 89.
[12] Rees, *Heritage,* 91.

brought face-to-face with an unalterable destiny" at that time.[13] And May Eve was more a day to celebrate the positive aspects of summer and the inevitable return to order, thus completing nature's cycle of life, death, and rebirth.

Not only borders between times of day or nature's cyclical seasons but also the physical boundaries dividing territories were considered "lines along which the supernatural intrudes through the surface of existence."[14] Rivers, creeks, property lines, and fences were all considered powerful border areas in Celtic belief.

In *The Hangman's Beautiful Daughter*, McCrumb writes of the importance of the mountains as a borderland. Because of these border characteristics, the mountains of Appalachia have always been viewed as a mystical place rife with superstition and mythology. Nora Bonesteel recognizes the importance of the mountains as borders in *The Hangman's Beautiful Daughter*. For Nora, "the mountains themselves were a border... They separate the placid coastal plain from the flatlands to the west, and there was magic in them."[15]

Rivers were also considered to have "the mysterious character of boundaries (which usually follows rivers and streams)." In *If Ever I Return, Pretty Peggy-O*, the French Broad River is the border between life and death for a murder victim. And in *She Walks These Hills*, McCrumb illustrates the boundary qualities of rivers when Jeremy Cobb encounters the spirit of the long-dead Katie Wyler near the banks of a river in McCrumb's fictional Wake County. During his long journey in search of Katie's spirit, he only hears her voice while on the banks of her native river—one by which she is believed to still roam. He feels the strength of this borderland as well as its blurring of time: "Soon it would be time to return to the twentieth century...here in the wilderness, devoid of temporal landmarks, he sometimes managed to find himself betwixt and between Katie's world and his own."[16] The Little Dove River in *The Hangman's Beautiful Daughter*, again the mystic border between this

---

[13] Rees, *Heritage* 91.

[14] Sharkey, *Mysteries*, 91.

[15] McCrumb, *Hangman*, 214.

[16] Sharyn McCrumb, *She Walks These Hills* (New York: Scribners, 1994) 251.

world and the Otherworld, is both the giver and taker of life. Not only has it nourished the land, but, because of the pollution caused by an upstream paper company, it thrusts one man to the borderland of cancer before crossing the final border into death. It also kills Laura Bruce's unborn child.

Nora Bonesteel recognizes the power of thresholds and borders as she collects balm of Gilead buds and the other plants and roots of herbal folk medicine. She knows the correct time to gather the buds for making salve, but she also knows the importance of other signs in showing when to begin her harvest. Generally collecting in the border twilight of early morning, Nora also uses other signs of nature to determine the best time to harvest the buds. "The balm of Gilead trees on Nora's land grew at the edge of the creek, so perhaps there was enchantment enough in that border, without their needing to be picked at the threshold of day to strengthen the charm."[17]

The forest acts as a borderland between the natural and spirit worlds in the *Rosewood Casket*. Both Kayla and a young Nora Bonesteel make contact with the spirit of a murdered child while playing in the woods. In *The Hangman's Beautiful Daughter* and *The Rosewood Casket*, Nora remembers old stories her grandmother told her of the Nunnehi, whose background reaches as far back as ancient Scotland where they were known as the seelie.[18] The Nunnehi and the seelie, who still inhabit the borderland of mountain forests and streams, were an important aspect of both Native American and Celtic mythology.

Another theme in Celtic myth, literature, and art, and one with ties to nature's cycles, is that of the triple goddess. In *Celtic Mysteries: The Ancient Religion*, John Sharkey points to the great number of "inscriptions to the Matronae, the Mother pictured as a triad" as proof of the importance of the triple goddess to the ancient Celts. She is a goddess of bounty but also a goddess of great power.[19] The triple goddess, seen as maiden, mother, and crone was the one "who presides over birth, life and

---

[17] McCrumb, *Hangman*, 214.
[18] McCrumb, *Hangman*, 7.
[19] Sharkey, *Mysteries*, 7.

death."[20] Further, she was considered the giver and taker of life.[21] In Greek mythology, she is Persephone, Demeter, and Hecate, and to the Celts she is Morrígan, Macha, and Badh.

In the Ballad series, McCrumb portrays the triple goddess as women who illustrate these three stages of life. These women are present and play significant roles in the lives of all who are affected by the relentless cycle of nature. The triple goddess appears in *If Ever I Return, Pretty Peggy-O* as the unmarried folksinger, Peggy Muryan; as Sheriff Arrowood's mother, Jane; and as Evelyn Johnson, a woman in the borderworld of Alzheimer's Disease, neither among the living nor the dead. Peggy represents the maiden aspect of the triple goddess, while Jane is the mother aspect. The crone, who usually symbolizes death, is Evelyn.

McCrumb illustrates this idea more clearly in the *Hangman's Beautiful Daughter*. These aspects of the cyclical nature of the triple goddess are seen in Maggie Underhill, a young girl just crossing the threshold into maturity; Laura Bruce, a mature woman on the brink of motherhood; and Nora Bonesteel, an aged woman who is herself a borderland between this world and the next. Maggie, the maiden, is a young woman entering womanhood whose potential in life is threatened by her family tragedy. Laura represents the fertile mother aspect of the triple goddess and, although her child dies before birth, she nevertheless becomes a mother through adoption. Nora Bonesteel, who has the gift of second sight, is the crone. Not only is she over seventy years old, but she often encounters those crossing the border between life and death.

In *She Walks These Hills*, McCrumb uses a young woman, Charlotte Pentland; her mother, Rita Pentland; and Nora to demonstrate the three aspects of the triple goddess. Nora herself is the triple goddess in the *Rosewood Casket*. Through the use of flashbacks, McCrumb presents Nora as a child, a young woman, and an old woman.

Finally, the most striking feature of Celtic mythology found in McCrumb's Ballad series is that of the second sight. The second sight is sometimes known as clairvoyance and is also identified with divination

---

[20] Sharkey, *Mysteries*, 7.
[21] Sharkey, *Mysteries*, 8.

and augury. *An dà shealladh* is Gaelic for second sight, and there is a "long tradition of people having second-sight experiences, especially in the Highlands and Western Isles of Scotland."[22] The Isle of Skye is well known for its inhabitants gifted with the second sight.

Second sight can be traced to the ancient druids, who were divided into three classes—druids, vates, and bards. The vates were linked with divination and eventually became known as seers and seeresses.[23] Although seers were generally thought to be men, Tacitus writes of seeresses as well. According to Tacitus, "they [the Celts] believe that there resides in women an element of holiness and a gift of prophecy."[24] Thus, mountain women, generally of Scottish descent, have become known for this gift, which is considered by many a burden rather than a gift.

Nora Bonesteel, who appears in all but one of McCrumb's Ballad series, is "gifted" with the Sight. Though not the main character, Nora's gift is essential to the working out of the plot in each novel. In *The Hangman's Beautiful Daughter*, Nora is the first to know of the Underhill family deaths as well as the death of Laura Bruce's unborn child. She has seen the spirit of Katie Wyler in *She Walks These Hills* and knows what no one else does—that Katie killed her own child. Randall Stargill, who is lying in a coma between life and death, appears to Nora as a vision in *The Rosewood Casket*. The spirit of young Fayre Stargill, too, has appeared to both the child and the adult Nora in this novel.

Some of the things Nora "knows" are coming births, sometimes before the expectant mother herself; recent deaths, often before they happen; and when to expect the start of winter. She also knows how to cure a variety of ills by quoting scripture or with natural medicine and when people are coming to visit before they arrive.

---

[22] Shari A. Cohn, "A Survey on Scottish Second Sight" *Journal of the Society for Psychical Research* 5 (1994): 386.

[23] Proinsias MacCana, *Celtic Mythology* (New York: Peter Bedrick Books, 1983) 12.

[24] H. R. Ellis Davidson, *Myths and Symbols in Pagan Europe: Early Scandinavian and Celtic Religions* (Syracuse: Syracuse University Press, 1998) 159.

Mythology is evident in McCrumb's novels even in the small details. The town of Hamelin has its own "trickster" in the form of Vernon Woolwine. Vernon, introduced in *If Ever I Return Pretty Peggy-O*, is a character who appears throughout the series and effectively provides this trickster element to the novels. No one knows what costume he will be wearing from day to day, and some of his costumes are surprisingly appropriate to town events, often mirroring or even presaging affairs of life and death. In *If Ever I Return, Pretty Peggy-O*, Sheriff Spencer Arrowood fears that Vernon may wear a Nazi uniform while the town honors its war dead on Memorial Day.

Greek mythology makes an appearance with Nora Bonesteel's pet groundhog named Persey for the mythological Persephone. Persey reminds Nora of the cycle of nature when she enters the earth for her winter hibernation. Nora looks forward each spring to the homecoming of her beloved pet because, like the mythological Persephone, Persey's return heralds the renewal of life. McCrumb's use of Persey also illustrates the cyclical nature of the world and its importance to Celtic myth.

Egyptian mythology, too, makes a brief appearance in *If Ever I Return, Pretty Peggy-O*. Martha, the sheriff's dispatcher and future deputy, considers her relationship with a Vietnam war veteran, who she feels has "been dead for a long time."[25] As she thinks about Joe LeDonne, she is reminded of the myth of Isis and Osiris, who fathered a child even after Osiris's death. This small scene demonstrates the way McCrumb seamlessly weaves mythology into her stories.

Through the many Celtic beliefs McCrumb has woven into her mountain stories, she has produced stories that are modern and, at the same time, as old as storytelling itself. Like mythology, these stories are timeless. Her themes echo those of the ancient Celts—the cycles of nature, the importance of boundaries, the triple goddess, and the second sight. These mythologies are as much a part of her novels as the setting and the characters themselves. They are the foundation on which McCrumb builds her characters and plots. McCrumb's work effectively

---

[25] Sharyn McCrumb, *If Ever I Return, Pretty Peggy-O* (New York: Balantine) 34.

demonstrates that mythology is not just a part of our past; it is a part of our present and future.

Gender, Class, and Regional Tradition in Sharyn McCrumb's *She Walks These Hills*

Tanya Mitchell

In a recent book on Appalachian women writers, *Bloodroot*, Joyce Dyer speaks about a "literary renaissance" that is taking place in Appalachia.[1] While she evokes the often-voiced complaint that women who have chosen to write with a sense of place have been virtually ignored by literary history, at the same time she also notices that regional writing has gained in popularity.[2] This increasing interest in regionalism is not only fostered by a wish to preserve the peculiarities of folk cultures, and it is not simply a return to organic concepts of nationhood on a smaller level in search of a new unity after the identity crisis generated by postmodernism, as some critics seem to suggest.[3]

---

[1] Sharyn McCrumb, "Keepers of the Legends" In *Bloodroot: Reflections on Place by Appalachian Women Writers,* ed. Joyce Dyer (Lexington: University of Kentucky Press, 1998) 1.

[2] McCrumb, *Bloodroot,* 1f.

[3] Dainotto, for example, sees the new regionalism in close connection to the Agrarian ideal of an organic community. Region in this sense suggests the possibility of a unity that is otherwise endangered by the breaking University Press of fixed concepts in the light of postmodernism. See Roberto Maria Dainotto, " 'All the Regions Do Smilingly Revolt:' The Literature of Place and Region," *Critical Inquiry* 22 (Spring 1996): 489.

A growing number of critics, among them David Jordan, have started to notice that "regionalism has recently begun to contribute a significant voice to some of the most urgent debates of our day."[4] For Jordan the subversive potential of regionalism consists in a decentered perspective on the world and on the dominant cultures.[5] In this sense it signifies a marginalized space. David Harvey in *Nature, Justice, and the Geography of Difference* develops this thought further. In his view, the world can either be seen as a "sphere which encompasses us or as a globe upon which we gaze."[6] The local perspective, to him, is just as important as the global one because it is place-bound experience and local knowledge which makes possible a "critical regionalism," one that cares for the environment and resists capitalist exploitation of underdeveloped regions.[7] Place is a "social construct" and thus can take on several meanings and functions.[8] Depending on the viewpoint, one can "look at places as the locus of 'imaginaries,' as 'institutionalizations,' as configurations of 'social relations,' as 'material practices,' as forms of 'power,' and as elements in 'discourse'."[9] In fiction or in the imaginary, which by nature lives from the space that it leaves for interpretation, place can take on all these meanings.

What divides the new regionalism from the older regionalist stance of the Agrarians is exactly this departure from the assumption of a region as a fixed concept of an authentic community. But what certainly links it to its predecessors is the fact that, although it offers "a forum for social protest," this social protest is bound to a sense of place.[10] And this sense of place is in some way always connected to feeling and experience. Eudora Welty in her famous essay "Place in Fiction" wrote that "fiction

---

[4] David Jordan, *Regionalism Reconsidered: New Approaches to the Field* (New York: University of Toronto Press, 1994) ix.

[5] Jordan, *New World Regionalism*, 8.

[6] David Harvey, *Justice, Nature, and the Geography of Difference* (Oxford: Blackwell, 1996) 37.

[7] Harvey, *Justice*, 306.

[8] Harvey, *Justice*, 293.

[9] Harvey, *Justice*, 294.

[10] Sherrie A. Inness and Diana Royer, eds., *Breaking Boundaries: New Perspectives on Women's Regional Writing* (Iowa City IA: University of Iowa Press, 1997) 1.

is bound up in the local" because "*feelings* are bound up in place"[11] and that "[l]ocation pertains to feeling; feeling profoundly pertains to place; place in history partakes of feeling, as feeling about history partakes of place."[12] With this she is not far from Raymond Williams' ideas of "living experience" and "structures of feeling." For Williams, feeling and thought are not separate, they belong together: "not feeling against thought, but thought as felt and feeling as thought."[13] By "living experience" he means social reality as well as the discourse about it. There is a part of social reality that cannot be transferred to theoretical consciousness:

> [T]here's a very vital area of social experience—social experience that doesn't get incorporated: that's neglected, ignored, certainly at times repressed; that even when it's taken up, to be processed or to function as official consciousness, is resistant, lively, still goes on its way, [...] It is from this vital area, from this structure of feeling that is lived and experienced but not quite yet arranged as institutions and ideas, from this common and inalienable life that I think all art is made.[14]

He posits a practical and a theoretical consciousness, whereby practical consciousness is "what is actually being lived" whereas theoretical consciousness is officially transmitted.[15] Changes in the structures of feeling come about through discrepancies in the relation between social experience and the given beliefs. Harvey accepts this premise and sees the active quest for a sense of place as a convergence of a present reflection over transmitted traditions that will open new ways

---

[11] Eudora Welty, "Place in Fiction," *A Modern Southern Reader*, eds. Ben Forkner and Patrick Samway, S.J. (Atlanta: Peachtree Publishers, 1986) 538, rpt. from *The Eye of the Story: Selected Essays and Reviews* (New York: 1956).

[12] Welty, "Place," 541.

[13] Raymond Williams, *Marxism and Literature* (Oxford: Oxford University Press, 1977) 131.

[14] Raymond Williams, *The English Novel From Dickens to Lawrence* (1970; London: Hogarth Press, 1984) 192.

[15] Williams, *Marxism and Literature*, 131.

into the future: "The preservation or construction of a sense of place is then an active moment in the passage from memory to hope, from past to future. And the reconstruction of places can reveal hidden memories that hold out the prospects for different futures."[16]

It can be argued that women's regional writing involves a subversive potential per se since from its beginnings it has presented the viewpoint of a marginalized group. Many nineteenth century local color writers were women, because, for them, the local color tradition opened directions toward liberation from the constraints of a patriarchal society in that it allowed them to break with the domestic conventions of the novel by depicting the local and the exotic. Additionally, it offered them a chance to earn their living through writing in a society where they had few other chances to lead a financially independent life. In fact, regional writing made marginality a positive asset because it focused on the poor and disenfranchised: "Through the inversion of customary privilege built into its logic this genre created a writer's role that women were equipped to perform, especially women from small towns and peripheral locations."[17] Women used the genre's conventions to express their critique of society, but they also transformed it and created their own literary regionalism.

Elizabeth Jane Harrison, for example, traces a line of a specifically female pastoral mode in Southern writing. One difference that she discerns in female pastoral writing is the fact that women writers, in contrast to many of their male counterparts, do not understand the land as something to be conquered but instead draw their identity from the land and in this portray land as an active force.[18] Many Southern and Appalachian women writers have connected place to the experience of freedom. In Appalachian literature, it was Mary Noailles Murfree who first set up a female identity that was closely linked to the land. As she wrote within the tradition of the domestic novel but at the same time

---

[16] Harvey, *Justice*, 306.

[17] Richard H. Broadhead, "Regionalism and the University Pressper Class," *Rethinking Class: Literary Studies and Social Formations*, eds. Wai Chee Dimmock and Michael T. Gilmore (New York: Columbia University Press, 1994) 151.

[18] Elizabeth Jane Harrison, *Female Pastoral: Women Writers Re-Visioning the American South* (Knoxville TN: University of Tennessee Press, 1991), 8f.

against it, she presents young heroines whose lives parallel the landscape. Connecting nature to virginity and to the sublime, her heroines stay single and are often immersed in the mountains. The men who come to the region destroy the women, and "Murfree thus suggests a destruction of the mountain world itself through contact with the outside world."[19] More than the New England local color writers, Murfree wrote with an awareness of class differences, a topic that became a strong component of almost all Appalachian literature to follow. Allen Batteau states that "[e]ven if the urbanite could not marry one of the rustic heroines of Murfree's stories, still it was a major step to afford these rustics the dignity of characterization in an otherwise genteel short story."[20] Thus, in Murfree's stories place, that is the mountains, signifies difference, a difference based on gender and class. To a certain extent this could be said about Sharyn McCrumb's Ballad novels as well. However, for the women in Murfree's stories the only chance of self-realization and escape from a patriarchal society is to be swallowed by the mountains and become one with nature. In Sharyn McCrumb's novels, a wider spectrum of social protest has become possible. Although the problem of personal freedom for women in a society with traditional gender and class structures is pervasive, she has also created some women characters who resolve this conflict.

In the following I will give an analysis of *She Walks These Hills* as social critique in respect to gender, class and regional tradition. The novel is the third sequel of a series called the Ballad novels. Formally, these novels could be categorized as detective fiction since the plot always develops loosely around a murder case. However, in contrast to the Elizabeth MacPherson Series (which features a woman amateur detective), the Ballad novels do not focus on a detective or police officer who solves the case. McCrumb herself has stated that whereas the MacPherson novels focus on plot, the Ballad novels concentrate on a theme. They give a portrayal of a whole community—Hamelin—in the

---

[19] Danny Miller, *Wingless Flights: Appalachian Women in Fiction* (Bowling Green OH: Bowling Green University Popular Press, 1996) 51.

[20] Allen Batteau, *The Invention of Appalachia* (Tuscon AZ: University of Arizona Press, 1990) 39.

Appalachian Mountains, whereby a variety of members of the community reappear in each novel. The community in all its diversity becomes the real protagonist.

She Walks These Hills, like the other Ballad novels, develops around several plot lines. An escaped convict tries to find his way home through the same wilderness area in which a history Ph.D. candidate is following the steps of a pioneer woman who escaped from captivity with the Shawnees. The main motif is the physical or spiritual journey home of almost all the characters in the book. Just as Hiram—or Harm—Sorley, the escaped convict, and Katie Wyler, the pioneer woman, try to make their literal journey home, so are police officer Martha Ayers, teenage mother Sabrina Harkryder, Ph.D. candidate Jeremy Cobb and Harm Sorley's former wife Rita Pentland and her daughter Charlotte in search of their identity. They all run into the wilderness of the Appalachian Mountains in order to find their true inner selves. Nature, respectively woman, the lower class and the Appalachian Mountains, are the marginalized spaces from where societal norms can be criticized.

Most of the women characters in the novel are presented as tragic victims of a traditional society, in which their gender as well as their class status leave them hardly any choices to decide about their lives. The only control that Katie Wyler and Sabrina Harkryder can exercise is the power over their children's lives. While Katie leaves her child with the Indians in order to save herself and get back to her fiancé, Sabrina sees her only chance of escape from a dreadful life as the wife of a trailer trash husband in the killing of her baby. When confronted with her deed, Sabrina says:

> 'I didn't exactly mean to [kill the baby]!' she said, staring into the fire. 'I just had to get away from there. I'm still a kid myself. I felt like a prisoner having to stay trapped up there in Painter Cove, missing my own people, and Tracy never paying me no mind. And it just kept crying all the time, day and night, crying, crying. I thought if I could just get shut of this kid, things could go back to being like they was before, and I'd be free to

leave. I could go back home to my mama, maybe even go back
to school. I never thought I'd miss it, but I did […].'[21]

On her escape into the wilderness Sabrina actually meets the ghost
of Katie Wyler as well as Charlotte Pentland, who, like her mother, is
searching for her real father Harm Sorley and thus finds a closer
connection to her mother's mountain roots and to her own Appalachian
identity. Sabrina also encounters Jeremy Cobb, a stereotype of the
politically correct scholar who finally awakens from his romantic notions
about Katie Wyler and her journey through the wilderness by
experiencing this journey through the wilderness himself and by meeting
the present-day version of Katie in the person of Sabrina. When Jeremy
tells Nora Bonesteel of his fascination with Katie and disrespectfully
considers Sabrina a hillbilly, the old woman points out the connection
between Katie and Sabrina under the aspects of gender and class: "Yes.
Not much education. No manners to speak of. Nothing much in the way
of looks or charm. Just a hard life that'll see her through just about any
trouble that comes. Katie all over again. She was a scrawny little thing,
too, all hair and eyes—and backbone, Katie was." Similar to the tragedy
of Sabrina's and Katie's experiences is the fate of Rita Pentland, Harm
Sorley's former wife, who has climbed up the social ladder with
marrying the well-respected Euell Pentland. Euell makes her feel that she
"started out as white trash" and after her disappearance comments that
"[h]er class doesn't observe the social niceties." Rita is murdered by him
because he cannot stand the thought that she would actually decide about
her own life and go back to her former "white trash" husband, just as
Katie Wyler is murdered by her fiancé because she decides that her life is
more important to her than her child's. Gender and class status also trap
Crystal Spangler, a waitress, for whom "[s]ex was the only bait she had"
to improve her life.

Nature or the wilderness means escape from the structures of society
for Katie, Sabrina, Rita and Charlotte Pentland, and Harm Sorley.
However, this escape is only a pseudo-escape where these characters find

---

[21] Sharyn McCrumb, *She Walks These Hills* (New York: Signet, 1994) 424. Further
references in parentheses in the text will be to this edition.

their inner selves for a short moment before they have to face the norms of society again. Nora Bonesteel tells Katie to go back to the Indians because going back to her culture means death for her. In the wilderness she can be free. Katie is a part of the wilderness: "Sometimes she seemed to be no more than a pin oak's shadow, or a trick of light among the leaves at dusk, so colorless silent was she among the trees." To Harm Sorley, who murdered his rich neighbor because he polluted his field, freedom appears in the form of spring and woman:

> Seasons didn't come behind the nicotine-stained white walls of Mountain City's prison, so Harm always imagined it spring—the locust trees shaggy with clustered white blooms, the wet woods flecked with bloodroot, and wild roses and honeysuckle flashing white among the chestnuts on the mountainsides. [...] He dreamed of golden fields of wild mustard, of snowmelt streams swirling around green trout pools, and of the taste of his mother's wild lettuce salad topped with spring onions and bacon drippings.

As a present-day version of the poor frontiersman who rebels against class structures by committing a crime against a rich man, he is the only man in the novel who shares his class status and his mountain roots with the women.

The woman who confronts society and finds a way to take control of her own life is police officer Martha Ayers. Like the other characters, she also runs into the wilderness, which is always a place freed of the "law of the fathers," and tries to find some comfort after her boyfriend Joe has betrayed her with Crystal: "When she walked the hills, she could think about what to do about that other matter." But unlike the others, Martha does not stay in the wilderness or get killed in it. She returns to society and confronts Joe. Martha takes on what is conventionally termed a man's game. Starting out as a dispatcher she is ambitious enough to apply for the job of deputy when the position becomes vacant. By taking the law into her own hands Martha risks losing her boyfriend and colleague, Deputy Joe LeDonne. He thinks that Martha tries to "outmacho him." In his hurt self-confidence he starts a sexual relationship with the waitress Crystal Spangler but he finally confesses to Martha: "'[…] I guess I wanted someone who'd be impressed by what I was doing, not somebody who was competing with me, matching my war stories with ones of her own.' Martha turned to look at him, her eyes narrowed. 'Is that your idea of a relationship, Joe? Quarterback and cheerleader?'" Martha faces the problems of a woman who does not want to comply with traditional role expectations in a male-dominated society. Two failed marriages have earned Martha the repudiation of not being a strong woman but rather of being unable to lead a so-called normal life, which in her environment means conforming to the ideal of submission. She therefore feels uncomfortable in how to deal with Joe's betrayal: "Spencer Arrowood would side with LeDonne, because men always stick together, and somehow all this would become *her* fault. Her family would offer no comfort. Martha had two failed marriages behind her: it was obvious to the Ayers clan that she just couldn't hold a man, so it was only natural that LeDonne should have strayed."

She perceives a bond with Sabrina Harkryder because, unlike herself, who was beaten by her first husband, Sabrina will not accept being mistreated. Having experiences with male violence, Martha seems to compensate for those experiences in her job. When Spencer Arrowood questions her abilities and claims that it might be dangerous for a woman to be a police officer, she counters that women are always in danger due to male violence. Thoughts about her job are often paired with reflections about male violence in the South:

A cold fact rose unbidden to Martha's mind: approximately 50 percent of all officers who were killed in the line of duty each year worked in the Southeast. […] It was a culture where guns and honor mixed to form a lethal combination for all concerned. […] [S]ome Southern men seemed to feel that Appomattox was the last insult their manhood would ever suffer. They fought authority at every turn, met every slight with clenched fists, and died to prove how brave they were. Some of them were outlaws, and some of them were cops. But almost all of them were male, and Martha thought that all of them were crazy. Gallant,

romantic, quixotic, courageous—maybe all of those things—but
doubly dangerous for all that, and no less crazy.

The other strong woman character in the Ballad novels is Nora
Bonesteel, the alter ego of the author. Nora lives alone in a cottage on a
mountaintop (the description of which resembles that of the author's
office in another Ballad novel). She exists outside the social order, in the
"wild zone," as Elaine Showalter has described the women's sphere in
her important essay "Feminist Criticism in the Wilderness."[22] In her role
as a seer she functions as a powerful figure out of women's folklore and
as an artist. The fact that she used to be a Sunday school teacher enforces
her role as a wise woman. She represents tradition, or more precisely the
hidden female side of tradition, and from this stance interprets history for
the community. As McCrumb has said in an interview with Rebecca
Laine: "She is the keeper of the legends. The woman who knew the quilt
patterns. She has all the treasures of our past in store."[23] Nora quilts and
weaves stories, sometimes stories that are still to come, thus realizing
author McCrumb's idea of her novels as Appalachian quilts. Patterns or
traces of the past or of the future are assembled and put together in a new
composition. In this sense Nora is the writer and the interpreter of the
history of a region and stands for the author. Meredith Sue Willis writes
that "McCrumb sometimes uses Nora and the Sight as a stand-in for the
writer—or perhaps she sees writing as a modern version of the Sight."[24]
Nora's visions can be understood as an approach to history and to writing
that is different from an objective, distanced historical approach in that it
emphasizes personal experiences and place over time. The basis for this
is a conception of time and space that Kristeva has thematized in her
essay "Women's Time."[25] For her, there is a difference between how

---

[22] Elaine Showalter, "Feminist Criticism in the Wilderness" *Critical Inquiry* 8
(Winter 1981): 179–205.
[23] Quoted in Rebecca Laine, "Telephone Interview with Sharyn McCrumb, July 8,
1997," 3 May 2000 <http://www.josephbeth.com/htm/mccrumbarchive.html>.
[24] Meredith Sue Willis, "The Ballads of Sharyn McCrumb" *Appalachian Journal*
25/3 (1998): 324.
[25] Julia Kristeva, "Women's Time," *The Kristeva Reader*, ed. Toril Moi (New
York: Columbia University Press, 1986) 160–86.

women and men perceive time and space. David Harvey, in referring to Kristeva'a essay, explains this difference with the different historical and social experiences that women and men have had:

> Under capitalism time gets construed quite differently according to gender roles through the curious habit of defining valued working time as only that taken up in selling labor power directly to others. [...] [T]he long confinement of a woman's world to the cyclical times of nature has had the effect of excluding women from the linear time of patriarchal history, rendering women "strangers in the world of male-defined time." The struggle, in this case, is to challenge the traditional world of myth, iconography, and ritual in which male dominion over time parallels dominion over nature and over women as "natural beings."[26]

For Kristeva, women's time has two components: cyclical time (repetition) and monumental time (eternity). "[W]hen evoking the name and destiny of women, one thinks more of the *space* generating and forming the human species than of *time*, becoming or history."[27] As Harvey claims, women's time is concerned with reproduction, which means (endless) rebirth, whereas linear time focuses on production and telos.[28] In this view, women's understanding of time is strongly connected to a personal, physical experience and this finds expression in a perception of history not as linear time but as place. "[T]ime and space are handled in a way that favors spatialized interruption rather than linear plot progression. Women's fiction progresses from the observable gesture of manners down to underlying mystery. This vertical dynamic offers the woman writer in an otherwise restricted world the potential for great movement in a small space."[29]

---

[26] Harvey, *Justice,* 226.

[27] Kristeva, "Women's Time," 190.

[28] Harvey, *Justice,* 226.

[29] Elizabeth A. Meese, "The Whole Truth: Frameworks for the Study of Women's Noncanonical Literature," *Teaching Women's Literature from a Regional Perspective,* eds. Leonore Hoffmann and Deborah Rosenfelt (New York: MLA, 1982) 21.

The pattern of *She Walks These Hills*—as in the other Ballad novels—is one of past events and themes repeating themselves in different versions in the present. Katie's story becomes Sabrina's stories; Rita Pentland's story becomes her daughter's story. While Kristeva sees the problematic of how to reconcile different conceptions of time and thus give women access to linear time, as well, McCrumb (or for that matter probably Harvey as well) brings out the at first sight hidden potential that this time-place conception has for a "critical regionalism."

For Nora, history is a psychic and therefore at the same time physical and epistemological experience because the Sight enables her to enter into contact with characters from the past and the future. She can feel Katie's anguish on her run through the wilderness. And it is Nora who explains Katie's and Sabrina's story for Jeremy Cobb and for the reader. She does this from a stance that not only sees the facts on the surface but that looks deeper into the minds of the women concerned. In this she reveals a story that would not appear in official historical records. It is part of the lived experiences of the characters involved. Raymond Williams claims that the "living experience" of a certain past cannot be transmitted because it does not get incorporated into theoretical consciousness. It is nonetheless resistant and alive. The great merit of art and of the artist is to recreate the structures of feeling of a certain period: "But while we may, in the study of a past period, separate out particular aspects of life, and treat them as if they were self-contained, it is obvious that this is only how they may be studied, not how they were experienced."[30]

"The structure of feeling, as I have been calling it, lies deeply embedded in our lives; it cannot be merely extracted and summarized; it is perhaps only in art [...] that it can be realized, and communicated, as a whole experience."[31]

In Nora Bonesteel's character Sharyn McCrumb gives us glimpses of the structure of feeling of another period. Nora re-lives history anew and this leads to revelations that are only possible on the level of

---

[30] Raymond Williams, *Drama in Performance* (London: Frederick Muller, 1954) 21f.

[31] Williams, *Drama,* 54.

personal bonding, such as when she interprets Katie's fate from a gender perspective. This personal bonding requires, as a basis, gender and class affinities as well as a shared (regional) tradition against or within which gender and class define the lives of the characters. Some of the other characters almost acquire Nora's Sight when they are in the wilderness of the Appalachian Mountains, for which Nora stands in a literal and metaphorical sense. Sabrina Harkryder, Jeremy Cobb, Harm Sorley and Charlotte Pentland all meet Katie Wyler at a critical point in their journeys home. Katie, who is, just like Nora, part of the wilderness and who is, like the others, on her way home, stands for the repressed memories of the region. Bringing these memories to the fore is what Sharyn McCrumb does in her novels.

In several interviews and essays she has made clear that she wants to convey a social message through her novels: "I try to write interesting, compelling stories because I think it is the duty of a fiction writer to entertain, but beyond the reader's concern for the characters, I want there to be an overlay of significance about the issues and the ambiguities that we face in Appalachia today. In my novels I want there to be truth and an enrichment of the reader's understanding of the mountains and their people. [...] I have a mission."[32]

Dyer sees this socio-historical and socio-political character as a distinctive feature in Appalachian women's fiction today. Unlike many other American writers, who see a "conflict between serving art and serving people," most Appalachian women writers explicitly link their art to the community.[33] By quilting or piecing together traces of the collective yet at the same time diverse past of the community and by arranging them in a new way, McCrumb reconstructs a new sense of history and of place and time, one that has as its main focus social justice. Region is not a closed concept but is shown in relation to factors like gender and class, a writing strategy which amounts to a complex understanding of regionalism as showing the (sometimes conflicting) forces on which a regional tradition grounds. *She Walks These Hills*

---

[32] Sharyn McCrumb, "Keepers," 186.
[33] Dyer, *Bloodroot,* 2.

displays a new regionalism, where the margin in the form of gender, class, and the local becomes the place of social critique.

The Old Ways

Nora Bonesteel in the Novels in Sharyn McCrumb's Ballad Series

Wanda Jared

Born in North Carolina, the descendent of preachers who traveled their circuits in the Smoky Mountains, Sharyn McCrumb has become one of this country's best-known novelists. The novels that have gained the most recognition are those in what is called the Ballad series because their titles come from ballads. They include *If Ever I Return, Pretty Peggy-O, The Hangman's Beautiful Daughter, She Walks These Hills, The Rosewood Casket,* and *The Ballad of Frankie Silver,* and *The Songcatcher.* The first two were named *New York Times* Notable Books and won between them the Best Appalachian Novel and the Macavity Awards. A *Los Angeles Times* reviewer says, "McCrumb draws you close, makes you care, leaves you with the sense…that what has gone has been not invention but experience recaptured."

In the Ballad series, the "experience recaptured" is the rural and small-town life of the mountains of the northeastern corner of Tennessee—just across the border from where McCrumb grew up. Here she creates the imaginary Wake County, Tennessee, with its county seat of Hamelin. McCrumb portrays the citizens of this county with what a *New York Times* book reviewer calls "quiet fire and maybe a little mountain magic." There are individuals like Jane Arrowood and her son, Spencer, the sheriff, whose ancestors lived there and who were born there themselves. They know most of the traditions of mountain life but do not see that they have any relevance in modern life. Spencer, in particular, questions their value. Despite the community's isolation, there are also outsiders such as Peggy Muryan, Joe LeDonne, and Laura Bruce who move in, bringing new ideas and different ways.

The character who holds most firmly to the old ways and practices is Nora Bonesteel. Nora is truly a "know-er"; she has the Sight. Since her childhood, she has seen things others cannot see. She knows what is going to happen before it happens. But her vision also extends back in time, allowing her to see individuals who are already dead and to know about their lives and what happened to them. The belief that some people are endowed with an ability to cross time and space and to have knowledge of the living and the dead is an old one, probably from "the descendants of that Celtic hearth culture" that migrated across Europe, eventually onto this continent, "taking with them fragments of the old beliefs" such as "the Sight."[1] According to legend, in the "east Tennessee hills, there have always been people who knew things.[2] While Nora is not a major character according to how much she appears in the novels, her presence, in keeping with the ballad titles, is similar to a background musical theme for whatever else is occurring.

Although these novels contain "mysteries," Nora does not use her power to help solve them. Neither does she use it to alter the course of events. She simply accepts it as a gift that enables her to protect or prepare her friends and neighbors. Like the ancestral traditions and beliefs that she knows and understands, Nora Bonesteel is there, in the midst of change and trouble, with her vision, making certain that the

---

[1] Sharyn McCrumb, *TheHangman's Beautiful Daughter* (New York: Scribners, 1992) 149.

[2] McCrumb, *Hangman*, 3.

traditions are followed and using her prescience to aid the people in the community.

At the time of the novels, Nora is an older woman, well into her 1970s. She lives alone on a mountain in Dark Hollow, outside of Hamelin, on property that has been in the Bonesteel family since 1793. She has known since she was a young child that she could see things that others couldn't see. By the time she is five, she understands that it is better not to talk about her gift because "it makes folks uneasy to have a little girl seeing things that aren't there."[3] When she is only seven, she smells smoke at a neighbor's house; a search reveals nothing. But two days later, the house burns, and her best friend Nellie, who lives there, dies in the fire.[4] When Nora talks about this episode with the minister's wife, newcomer Laura Bruce, Laura asks Nora if she feels guilty because she was not able to prevent Nellie's death. But Nora has learned to accept the limitations of her gift, adding that after the fire Nellie came to her and told her that it was not her fault. Interestingly Nellie continues to appear to Nora until Nora grows up, suggesting that some degree of her gift is tied to the innocence of childhood.

As a child, Nora does not understand the gift she possesses. No one tells her that she is "marked" or "blessed" in any way. She simply learns from what happens. She goes on the first of what she calls "excursions" before she is six.[5] In these episodes, the time period changes—maybe only for a moment—and Nora finds herself in a time and place other than the one she actually exists in. Her Grandma Flossie, who also possesses the Sight, calls this "stray [ing] a little from the path of time."[6] After the first excursion, Nora tries to do it deliberately, but that never happens. The shift always comes unexpectedly and while the episodes do not stop the way Nellie's appearances do, they come "less frequently as Nora grows older."[7] Nora speculates that the excursions are somehow linked to the mind of a child who can concentrate totally on something without having the "steady drumbeat of adult obligations" keeping her on the

---

[3] Sharyn McCrumb, *The Rosewood Casket* (New York: Dutton, 1996) 50.

[4] McCrumb, *Hangman*, 18–19.

[5] McCrumb, *Hangman*, 168–70.

[6] McCrumb, *Hangman*, 170.

[7] McCrumb, *Hangman*, 170.

time path.[8] So some expressions of Nora's gift diminish or leave her completely as she matures. Nora's acceptance of her gift suggests that somehow it endows her with a maturity and perceptiveness beyond her years. She is ten before she fully comprehends that she can see objects, people, and places that others cannot. But once she thinks it through, she decides that "most folks see only what is here and now, but that she can see what was and what is going to be. She doesn't know why she was made different, but she figures that was the Lord's business, not hers, and if He wanted to do something with it, He'd let her know."[9] So on her own, Nora decides not to mention things she sees such as "funeral wreaths and cloth-draped mirrors" until she touches them and knows they are real."[10]

Nora's gift of the Sight is somewhat different from what other individuals possess. Many mountain families have members who possess the "simple gifts" of knowing when a frost will come, how to cure nosebleeds by quoting from the Bible, how to gauge the severity of a coming winter, or when a relative will die.[11] Similar to Nora, other characters in the novels hear or see individuals who are dead. In *She Walks These Hills*, Jeremy Cobb and Sabrina Harkryder hear Katie Wyler guiding them. In the *Rosewood Casket*, the child Kayla sees the dead child Fayre. All three individuals, however, are physically lost at the time of the appearance and have a special bond with the dead person that causes her to appear. Jeremy Cobb, who has devoted his life to learning about Katie Wyler, is attempting to imitate her escape route. Sabrina killed her own baby, just as Katie did. Like Fayre, Kayla is a child caught in adult conflicts and endangered by an adult. But the appearances of the dead to these characters are one-time happenings, limited to special circumstances. Nora's gift is not limited by circumstances and is more extensive that just a knowledge of the old practices. She knows all of these and more: "it isn't only a matter of knowing about close kin. The fate of the whole community seems as

---

[8] McCrumb, *Hangman*, 170.
[9] Sharyn McCrumb, *She Walks These Hills* (New York: Scribners, 1994) 2.
[10] McCrumb, *Walks*, 2.
[11] McCrumb, *Hangman,* 2.

open to her as the weekly newspaper. Even newcomers,…and outsiders,…are within the range of her visions."[12] Even with her greater knowledge, Nora says more than once, "The Sight never tells me anything I want to know."[13] And like the excursions, the different manifestations of her gift come to her unbidden. She cannot cause them to happen.

While the Sight is the most exceptional manifestation of Nora's gift, it is not the only one. She does possess the more common abilities of many others, and they are part of the old mountain lore that she tries to maintain. When her friend Geneva Albright dies, Nora makes no plans to attend her funeral. No one expects her to because she does not attend funerals. Knowing Geneva's children and grandchildren "have been brought up as city children" and do not know "the old ways of attending to a death," she volunteers to stay at Geneva's house while the family is at the church.[14] She knows her old friend would want her to do what to them is "right."[15] So during the funeral Nora observes these "old ways of attending death":

> she puts the jar of honey away, so that no one will eat any without thinking. You didn't eat honey on the day of a funeral. That done, she turns to the more important duties of a death in the house. She stops all the clocks in the cottage, and opens all the doors and windows. It is August; she can tell Junior and Tessa that she was airing things out before company started arriving. She doubts they will notice the tin cup of salt she sets on the windowsill and they will think Geneva's silk scarf has fallen across her bedroom window by happenstance. She won't tell them otherwise.[16]

After she completes these routine tasks, she goes to tell Geneva's bees of her death because, according to tradition, if she doesn't tell them

---

[12] McCrumb, *Hangman*, 3.
[13] McCrumb , *Hangman*, 151.
[14] McCrumb, *Walks,* 101.
[15] McCrumb, *Walks,* 102.
[16] McCrumb, *Walks,* 102.

of their keeper's death, they will take flight and no one will want them. As she walks toward the hive carrying a black ribbon, she chants: "Stay pretty bees, and fly not hence. Geneva Albright is dead and gone."[17] Without any longer understanding why these rituals of mourning are important, Nora believes they are and observes them for her friend. As she moves around her friend's property, she is consoled because she doesn't feel a sense of Geneva's presence, indicating that Geneva is truly gone, that she was ready to go, and that she has already arrived wherever she was going. Nora concludes that Geneva's death is "a release and a beginning, rather than a tragedy."[18]

Some of the citizens of Wake County want to keep their distance from Nora, saying that friendship with her would be "like having Death as an upstairs boarder."[19] When Randall Stargill and Nora are young, Randall is so disturbed by Nora's gift that he marries someone else—someone who sees only what is real.[20] But most of her neighbors see her as benevolent, one who wishes no harm. She has taught the young teenagers in Sunday school for many years. When she does have a warning to give, her neighbors know that she will "look away...and say what she has to say in a sorrowful way that is nobody's idea of a curse."[21] In fact, most of them are sorry for her, relieved that they can live "with the hope that comes from not seeing the future through well-polished glass."[22]

Occasionally Nora does give warnings of sorrow or danger to come. Sometimes the warnings are to prepare an individual for what is to happen. But the warnings are rarely explicit. At the time Nora receives the knowledge, she may not understand the warning. She says, "Sometimes I can't make out what they [the warnings]...mean until what they foretell goes and happens."[23] In effect, the knowledge may simply prepare the person to accept what is to happen after it happens, not

---

[17] McCrumb, *Walks*, 102.
[18] McCrumb, *Walks*, 103.
[19] McCrumb, *Hangman*, 83.
[20] McCrumb, *Hangman*, 147.
[21] McCrumb, *Rosewood*, 3.
[22] McCrumb, *Hangman*, 3.
[23] McCrumb, *Hangman*, 18.

before. For example, when Laura Bruce asks Nora to knit something for the baby Laura expects in April, Nora "carefully [untangles] a knot of crimson wool and says, 'I will make you something for the child you will have in April.'"[24] Instead of telling Laura that the child she is carrying will be born dead, Nora holds out hope by referring to the child Laura will have—the motherless child she will take as her own. Later Laura is angry because Nora did not tell her the exact truth, but then she realizes that, as Nora says, "Knowing is one thing. Changing is another."[25] Nora's nebulous warning helps prepare Laura to accept what she cannot change.

In another instance, Nora's warning is definitely intended to protect. When she tells Jane Arrowood to tell her son to "be careful—of old friends,"[26] the words are too general to be of much value to Spencer. As sheriff in a small county, he is surrounded by old friends. And when the moment comes that Nora refers to, Spencer reacts as any law enforcement officer would. He tackles the intended target of the bullet, putting himself in its path. Despite the warning, he does what he has to do and takes the bullet himself. After all, he is the sheriff, and taking care of others is his job. Nora probably sums up her situation best when she tells Laura that "Most things aren't meant for us to know beforehand."[27] Even knowing, Nora Bonesteel does not alter the course of events.

As sheriff, Spencer is not just skeptical about Nora's gift, he feels that "such things have no place in his world of order and law and finding probable cause."[28] When she does possess the knowledge he needs, she refuses to tell him if revealing it will hurt someone. In the *Rosewood Casket*, she resists telling Spencer the story of the bones in the box until Randall Stargill is dead and can no longer be held responsible for what he knew as a child. Occasionally Spencer sees the similarity in his and Nora's relationships with others. When he notes how anxious and uneasy he makes people, he realizes that it is because they see him as a messenger of death and speculates that Nora probably feels the same

[24] McCrumb, *Hangman*, 60.
[25] McCrumb, *Hangman*, 304.
[26] McCrumb,, *Rosewood*, 182.
[27] McCrumb, *Hangman*, 59.
[28] McCrumb, *Hangman*, 45.

reaction.[29] And he acknowledges that they have both seen enough of deceit and tragedy to understand that "The whole truth is something very few of us want to hear."[30]

Nora Bonesteel does not even appear as a character in *If Ever I Return, Pretty Peggy-O*. She appears on only twenty pages in *She Walks These Hills* and *The Hangman's Beautiful Daughter*, and her contributions to the "mysteries" in these two novels do not directly solve them. Only in *The Rosewood Casket*, where she appears on approximately forty pages, does she possess conclusive knowledge that aids the sheriff in solving his case. Does the author's increasing use of her character suggest that she plans to focus more on her? Possibly. But no character is the traditional main character in these novels, not even Spencer even though he is the sheriff. The story is the most important element in each novel. What then does Nora's character contribute to the novels? She is not there to threaten or intimidate the people of Wake County. Instead she uses her gift of the Sight and her knowledge of the old practices to help and protect them. Nora Bonesteel is in their background, their heritage of a different time, a different place, when their ancestors understood that, as Pinero says, "the future is simply the past, entered through another gate."

[29] McCrumb, *Hungman, 112*.
[30] McCrumb, *Rosewood,* 296.

Melungeons in McCrumb's Fiction

Katherine Vande Brake

New York Times best-selling writer Sharyn McCrumb, born in North Carolina and now living in Southwest Virginia, writes about the mountains and towns of Appalachia because she knows them like the back of her hand. Her characters drive to Johnson City and Bristol, go to rock concerts in Knoxville, go to college and graduate school at East Tennessee State or Virginia Tech, and talk about country music and Melungeons. McCrumb weaves the passions and the prejudices of the region into every book she writes. McCrumb's Ballad novels use familiar Appalachian legends—ballads—in stories of suspense and intrigue. The primary characters in each one of the ballad series are Sheriff Spencer Arrowood and his deputies Joe LeDonne and Martha Ayers. These three have at least one major law enforcement problem to solve in each book. Another series, the Elizabeth McPherson novels, features the adventures of a forensic anthropologist. Critics praise McCrumb's ability to cross genres and explore new ground and call her "versatile;" she is known for giving the Appalachian region a memorable voice in contemporary fiction. McCrumb has written two books that feature Melungeon characters.

She Walks These Hills (1994), one of the Ballad novels, is a multi-layered narrative that uses the theme of journeys. It is built around the mountain story of Katie Wyler (fictional but partially based on a real person, Mary Draper Ingalls), a young woman captured by Indians, who manages to escape and walk from Pennsylvania back to Northeast Tennessee by following the rivers and the mountain ridges. Many others in the narrative are on journeys of their own: Harm Sorley, a sixty-three-year-old mentally ill murderer, has escaped from NECC in Mountain City and is heading home in the same manner as Katie Wyler; Jeremy Cobb, a history grad student at Virginia Tech is backpacking to re-create for himself a part of Katie's journey; Martha Ayers, the dispatcher in the Wake County Sheriff's office is determined to succeed as a deputy when given a chance—her journey toward vocational fulfillment; Rita Sorley Pentland vows to return to the remote mountain clearing where she lived when Harm left her to go to prison; her daughter Charlarty is forced to go from denying and intellectualizing her mountain heritage to acknowledging and cherishing it; and Sabrina Harkryder, the Melungeon in the story, journeys from a pinched adolescence to a bleak adulthood.

We are told of Sabrina's blood heritage the first time we meet her after her hardscrabble Harkryder in-laws have called the sheriff because Sabrina has threatened to kill her infant son, Dustin Allison Harkryder (named after NASCAR driver Davey Allison). The baby's grandfather says, "'I told that boy not to marry her. She's got Melungeon blood. Ain't no telling what them folk will do, I said to him.'"[1] Not only is Sabrina threatening to kill her baby, but she has poisoned all the Harkryder hounds by lacing their food with anti-freeze. As Deputy Martha Ayers approaches Sabrina and hears the story, we learn that Sabrina got pregnant, dropped out of school to marry Tracy Harkryder, and has pretty much been abandoned by him in the tumble down trailer in Painter (as in "panther") Cove:

> [A]s soon as I started getting all fat and tired, he wouldn't give me the time of day! He was always off somewheres cruising with his buddies, staying out half the night. You know where he was the night the kid was born? At a damned Alan Jackson concert in Knoxville!….After the baby come, I had stitches from where they cut me down there, so I couldn't do nothing, and Tracy kept griping about how he'd been without his rights for

[1]Sharyn McCrumb, *She Walks These Hills* (1994, New York: Signet, 1995) 114.

such a long time. So he went out and found some bitch to give it to him. He told me last night. Said he'd be back today to get his clothes and his stereo."[2]

Sabrina goes on to tell that she thought threatening to kill the baby might get Tracy to pay attention to her. However, her ploy doesn't work. As she says, "'He didn't care, though. I reckon he loved them damned dogs better than us.'"[3]

Sabrina's story is laced throughout McCrumb's narrative. We see her again bruised and miserable at a high school football game, and then near the end of the novel she appears at the Sheriff's office to report that her baby is missing. "'Sheriff,' she said. 'That there convict stole my baby. I want you to shoot him down like a dog.'"[4] Spencer Arrowood has no choice but to drive up to Painter Cove to begin searching for the baby. Sabrina is coldly silent most of the trip except for occasional angry outbursts: "'I don't think Tracy would have bothered to take Dustin Allison if the damned trailer had been on fire... It's not like anybody helps me or anything. I take care of him (the baby) round the clock, you know.'"[5] Spencer searches the cold and filthy trailer and asks Sabrina the usual questions while he waits for the search party of volunteers to arrive on the mountain.

One of the Harkryder women appears to talk with the Sheriff. "Her lank hair was iron gray, and her face was quilted with fine lines around the eyes and mouth. She looked sixty; Spencer doubted she was much past thirty-five."[6] Her words to Spencer add to the sense of impending doom that the gray cold day and the poverty of Painter Cove have already created, "'When that Sabrina planted parsley in her garden plot, I told her she ought not to do it, because parsley in a yard invites death into the house, and she was pregnant then, but when I warned her, she just back-talked me, and went on planting. It was a sign; I knowed right

---

[2]McCrumb, *Hills*, 118.
[3]McCrumb, *Hills*, 119.
[4]McCrumb, *Hills*, 348.
[5]McCrumb, *Hills*, 354–55.
[6]McCrumb, *Hills*, 363.

then it was. That poor little baby. You won't find h'it alive.'"[7] Spencer himself is the one who finds the baby's body: "The sheriff stared at the log for nearly a minute before he realized what was wrong with it... The bark on the top side of the locust was damp, although it hadn't rained in the last twenty-four hours....he saw what [the log] had been intended to conceal; a two-foot rectangle of broken soil.... His fingers touched something that wasn't dirt, the pale roundness of a tiny fist beneath his hand."[8]

When Spencer goes back to the patrol car, the search party is in a state of angry disbelief not because they know about the baby, but because Sabrina has stolen a vehicle belonging to one of them.

Sabrina quickly abandons the car after she manages to get it stuck in mud and meets up with Jeremy Cobb, who by this time is footsore, cold, and hungry. Although not dressed for the cold or the hard terrain, it is obvious that Sabrina could survive in the wilderness—like Katie Wyler. Jeremy tells Sabrina Katie's story and asks her what she thinks about the fact that Katie's fiancé, Rab Greer, apparently killed Katie when she returned from her incarceration with the Shawnees. Sabrina refuses to pass judgment on either Rab or Katie "'I think people can get caught between a rock and a hard place, and then there's no right answers without someday getting hurt,'" she says.[9]

Of course this response is prophetic because by this time the reader may have already guessed that Sabrina has murdered her own child just as Katie Wyler murdered the child she was carrying when she was captured. Both Katie and Sabrina realize they will not be able to survive themselves with the very real burden of an infant and decide that personal survival is more important. Readers don't learn this information outright until the very end of the novel when Sabrina has led Jeremy on his bleeding feet to seer Nora Bonesteel's house high on Ashe Mountain. Nora, who sees things that others do not, has had encounters with Katie's ghost since childhood and uncannily knows many things before they happen. Nora realizes that Sabrina and Jeremy have seen Katie and heard

---

[7]McCrumb, *Hills,* 364.
[8]McCrumb, *Hills,* 372–73.
[9]McCrumb, *Hills,* 394.

her voice even before Sabrina confirms it. "'Yeah,' [says Sabrina] 'I heard it. First we smelled smoke and heard a lot of yelling, then we heard somebody come up and tell us to run. It didn't bother me. I know about spirits and such. I'm Melungeon, you know.'"[10]

> Nora, who has known for many years that Katie Wyler killed her baby so that she could escape from the Indians and begin her trek home, elicits the parallel truth from Sabrina. 'I didn't exactly mean to!... I felt like a prisoner having to stay trapped up there in Painter Cove, missing my own people, and Tracy never paying me no mind. And it just kept crying all the time, day and night, crying. I thought if I could just get shut of this kid, things could go back to being like they was before, and I'd be free to leave. I could go back home to my mama, maybe even go back to school. I never thought I'd miss it but I did.'[11]

This resolution is shocking and brutal. Katie was certainly in extreme circumstances. Sabrina is too; however, many girls have married immature and abusive men to legitimize a pregnancy and made it through without killing their babies. The thing that seems if not to justify then to explain Dustin Allison's murder is the fact that Sabrina is Melungeon and, as we have already been told, "'ain't no telling what them folk will do.'"[12]

Readers are not told much about Melungeons or their heritage in this novel. There is an explanatory paragraph early when readers first meet Sabrina. "The Melungeons were an olive-skinned people of uncertain origin who had lived in the northeast Tennessee mountains for generations. Depending on who you asked, they were a lost tribe of Indian, descendants of Portuguese explorers, or the offspring of runaway slaves. Nobody knew for sure, and mostly they kept to themselves."[13] As a reader I feel sorry for Sabrina Harkryder—she is between a rock and a

---

[10]McCrumb, *Hills*, 423.
[11]McCrumb, *Hills*, 424.
[12]McCrumb, *Hills*, 119.
[13]McCrumb, *Hills*, 114.

hard place—but I do not condone her actions, nor do I think that the apparent explanation is sufficient. I tend to fault her Harkryder in-laws as much or more than her Melungeon heritage. The other women in Painter Cove could/should have at least tried to mitigate her loneliness and supported her in her new roles as wife and mother. Even though the situation for them was far from ideal, they knew the code and had themselves survived under the same circumstances. But, of course, they are Harkryders, if only by marriage; and, once a reader gets into McCrumb's Ballad novels, she knows that Harkryders are not redeemable.

Lovely in Her Bones (1985) is one of McCrumb's "Elizabeth McPherson" novels. Readers get the clues to the resolution of two murders as the characters get them; we are just slower to figure everything out than Elizabeth. Before the novel ever begins there is a note from the author acknowledging her real debts to persons who helped her in her research from the fields of forensic anthropology and Appalachian studies; she then goes on to say "The Cullowhees are based on several groups of 'racial isolates' in Appalachia and elsewhere, and their social and political situation is consistent with the actual experiences of some of these groups."[14]

As I read I surmised that McCrumb had read Jean Patterson Bible's book. This supposition has since been confirmed in an email from McCrumb herself. She said that she also used material from the outdoor drama *Walk Toward the Sunset* as a resource. The word Melungeon is never used in the novel, but the "racial isolates" phrase at the beginning is both a clue to her intent and her position on the issue of Melungeon origins, at least when she wrote this novel back in the mid 1980s.

As the novel opens Comfrey Stecoah, a representative of a group of people (perhaps a lost Indian tribe?), approaches one Dr. Alex Lerche, a forensic anthropologist at Virginia Tech. Lerche's big project is a complex chart that classifies skulls into racial groups by exact measuring of certain characteristics. Lerche has worked in the past with Plains Indians but is eager for more data. Stecoah's group of people who live in isolated Sarvice Valley call themselves Cullowhee Indians and are

---

[14]Sharyn McCrumb, *Lovely in Her Bones* (New York: Ballantine, 1985) 5.

seeking tribal status from the US Government for the financial benefits that status would confer and are being threatened by a strip-mining operation. Stecoah offers to let the anthropologists dig up a graveyard and prove the group's right to tribal status by the skull measurements.

Stecoah arranges for the team of experts to camp in a valley Baptist church, and their time in the valley commences with a covered dish dinner and a lecture by Dr. Lerche. The dig itself is staffed by Lerche, two grad students in anthropology, two undergrads, some faceless diggers who drive in every day, and Elizabeth McPherson. Elizabeth's connection is not professional; although she is mildly interested in anthropology, her real interest is Milo, one of the grad students. Elizabeth's task on the dig is to take the measurements of the skulls. Lerche and Milo set up a computer in a motel room in nearby Laurel Cove in order to have access to the figures already entered on Lerche's chart. Early on the motel room is ransacked and the computer and all the relevant disks are destroyed. This alerts the team of workers to the fact that not every one of the Cullowhees is on board with Stecoah's plan. Just as they are recovering from this destruction (a trip back to the university for another computer and for replacement disks puts them back in business) Lerche is murdered with a "play" tomahawk. Stunned, but undaunted, Milo, who is next in command, vows to continue in memory of the fallen leader. Shortly after Lerche's murder, Victor Bassington, the more disagreeable of the two undergrad students, dies mysteriously on his way from the dig site to the church to refill the water jug.

All work on the dig stops. Elizabeth and Jake Adair, the second of the undergrads, are confined to the church for safety's sake and begin talking. Elizabeth learns that Jake is a full blood Cherokee. Jake tells her among other things that the word "unaka" is the Cherokee word for "white man." This is the clue that unlocks the mystery for her. Elizabeth has taken a course in herb lore. As soon as she arrives in Sarvice Valley, she visits Amelanchier Stecoah, Comfrey's mother who is known as "The Wise Woman of the Woods." Amelanchier tells Elizabeth that the Cullowhees claim descent from the Unaka Indians, but sadly they have lost all their traditions, language, and folklore. This, coupled with the fact that the skull measurements do not match the data from the skulls of

Plains Indians, shows Elizabeth that Amelanchier is the murderer. Elizabeth deduces correctly that Amelanchier knows that the Cullowhees are not Indians and fears that truth will come out from the anthropologic study and ruin their chances for tribal status. Elizabeth sends Jake out to get tomatoes for lunch and hikes through the woods alone to confront Amelanchier, who admits the crimes while feeding Elizabeth poison in a mug of tea. Milo and Comfrey arrive in time to rush Elizabeth to the hospital. Everybody still alive at this point in the novel lives happily ever after.

There are many references in this novel to the realities of life for an isolated people group that stem from McCrumb's obvious research into that situation and other related subjects. During Stecoah's first visit to Dr. Lerche's office at the university, he says,

> The trouble is can't nobody agree on where we came from. Some people want to think we're descended from the Indians and settlers of the Lost Colony, but I don't believe it. That was all the way across North Carolina on the coast. We're mountain people. My mother claims we're descended from a tribe called the Unakas who intermarried with some Moravian missionaries from Salem. Then there's folk who claim some of Daniel Boone's people left the party around the Cumberland Gap, and that they moved in with the local tribe, and that we're the descendants of that mixture. It don't matter a hill of beans to me, as long as we get the land.[15]

The characteristic mixture of possible phenotypes in Melungeon groups is described in the book as Lerche looks at the people who have come to the church for the covered dish supper. "[H]e studied their features; green eyes, brown eyes, dark hair of every variation, every shape of face. The Cullowhees couldn't have been as isolated as they seemed."[16] This characteristic comes up again when Jake and Elizabeth are looking at old photographs of Cullowhees that are displayed in the

---

[15]McCrumb, *Bones,* 37.
[16]McCrumb, *Bones,* 61.

church Sunday school room they are living in. Elizabeth, looking at a sepia photo of a bygone Sunday school class, exclaims, "'...they're just as much of a hodge-podge as the ones today. Blonds, people with dark straight hair, people with dark kinky hair, light ones, dark ones.'"[17]

There is a reference to the tendency toward moonshining as a vocation, or avocation. "The Cullowhee Indians of Sarvice Valley had never been a particularly law-abiding group, and they were known for moonshining."[18] The idea that "these people"—Melungeons in *She Walks These Hills*, Cullowhees in this one—can behave in strange and unpredictable ways is also present. "Pilot [the deputy sheriff] could well believe that there had been trouble in Sarvice Valley; the Cullowhees were an ornery bunch of folks, and trouble would be no stranger to that hollow of theirs. It seemed feasible that they had bashed somebody's head in for any number of reasons: poker game, drunk fight, that strip-mining business."[19]

Later Pilot explains the trait for mischief to the FBI man who comes to help with the murder investigation:

> Take the Cullowhees, for instance. Those folks are so mean they must've been weaned on snake venom. Ain't a man in the valley that hasn't seen the inside of our jail two or three times. Summer's the worst. They get so likkered up they stab their own mothers" [Pilot goes on to narrate a well-known Cullowhee story]. 'Bunch of Cullowhees got piss-eyed drunk at a poker game up here and killed some joker they claimed was cheating. He was a white man, too. Lord knows how he got in the game in the first place...Well, they stabbed him in the belly, and went on with the game while he bled to death. And then they strung him up in chains behind a pickup truck and drug him down the highway to Laurel Cove.... There was about ten of them, a-sitting in the back of that pickup, waving like it was the Easter parade.... They got the driver of the truck by his license number,

---

[17]McCrumb, *Bones,* 78–79.
[18]McCrumb, *Bones,* 66.
[19]McCrumb, *Bones,* 105.

but he claimed not to remember who the others were. Never did charge anybody with the murder.[20]

The FBI man asks who the Cullowhees really are and Pilot responds, "'People say they're part Portuguese or African or Inca. I've heard they're descendants of the Lost Colony.'...[A second deputy adds,] 'Nobody knows who they're related to, but the devil himself is related to them.'"[21]

Particular brands of Christianity are hinted at when Deputy Pilot Barnes comes out to Sarvice Valley to investigate Lerche's murder; he must use the Baptist church sanctuary for an interrogation room. As he looks it over he carries on an internal monologue. "He'd wondered if the Cullowhees were footwashers or snake handlers, but seeing the sanctuary he reckoned not."[22]

As noted in the plot outline, Elizabeth pursues her interest in herb lore by making a visit to Amelanchier Stecoah's log cabin quite soon after the diggers arrive in the valley. The old woman tells the young one stories about the origin of the Cullowhee people.

> Most of the county was Cullowhee land in the old days...Flat land you could farm, down on the creek bottoms. But then the whites came in wanting land, and they reckoned to steal it... If we had been regular old Indians, why, there wouldn't have been no trick to it at all. They would have marched us out to the desert, like they did the Cherokees—but we were different. Here we was a-talking English, living in regular old cabins, and praying to Jesus, just same as them. There was only one difference.' The old woman pressed her gnarled brown arm against Elizabeth's white one. 'They called us people of color, and said we didn't have no rights. Got a law passed at the state capitol saying we couldn't vote nor hold office. Hell, we couldn't even testify in a court of law...Then they started in with

[20]McCrumb, *Bones,* 154.
[21]McCrumb, *Bones,* 154.
[22]McCrumb, *Bones,* 140–41.

their lawyers and their judges, and they stole all the farmland away from our 'The law is gone, but the feeling stayed here right on.'...Elizabeth shivered. Even in August it was not really warm on the mountain. The wind under the oaks bore the chill of autumn. Amelanchier sat still in her faded sundress, staring out at the mountains. After a while, she continued. 'No, the feelings ain't gone. When my young'uns were little, we'd go into town and I could buy them a sody pop at the grill, but they'd have to stand outside to drink it.[23]

The old woman goes on to recount another sinister form of prejudice that Melungeons and other isolate groups endured. She asks Elizabeth a question and goes on to give the answer. "'Why do you think I'm a root doctor?...The Cullowhees always had a root doctor because no town doctor would see our people. It was passed down from my gran'daddy to me, because I was the seventh of his seventh child. Some things we can't cure, and folks dies. But we did what we could, which is more than the white folks would."[24]

There is no more information given explicitly until the end of the novel after Elizabeth has figured out that Amelanchier has committed the murders in order to suppress the fact that the Cullowhees are not real Indians after all. Elizabeth asks the old woman,

'Who are you really? Does anybody know?'

'Only me. I'm the oldest one alive, so I remember when folks knew. My grandfather still had the whip scars on his back.'

'You were slaves then? Run away from plantations?'

'Sold from the plantations,' said Amelanchier in a steady voice. 'Run away from the Cherokees.... my people didn't go [on the Trail of Tears]. They run off and came back to the hills. Been here ever since. Most of 'em was half-breeds, mixed black and white.'

'But why did you claim to be Indian?'

---

[23]McCrumb, *Bones,* 140–41.
[24]McCrumb, *Bones,* 141.

'Because between 1830 and very recently, being anything else was not healthy around here. If they'd said they were black, they could'a been took back in slavery till the War between the States, and even after that they was worse off than the Indians.'

'But everyone knows you weren't really Indian?

'It was my gran'daddy, the Wise Man, who changed that. When I was a little bitty girl, he told folks that the best way to keep a secret is not to tell it out, so from then on, the children were told they was real Indians. When I go, the truth goes with me; I never told a one of my young'uns any different. I never knowed you could tell from the ones of the dead.'[25]

Discerning readers can tell where McCrumb got her information by the slant she chooses to take on origins. One theory in Bible's book is that the Goins line of Melungeons that settled in Blackwater just below Newman's Ridge in Hancock County Tennessee and Lee County Virginia did descend from escaped slaves. The part about the Cherokees may be original to McCrumb, although her telling that the Cherokees did adopt many "white" practices including the owning of slaves in Georgia is entirely correct.

The whole plot of *Lovely in Her Bones* turns on the determination of the old woman and her disregard for both the lives of outsiders and the law. Brent Kennedy and others have commented on how Melungeons themselves suppressed true information about origins and history even within families to protect the younger generations as much as possible from the ravages of unfair laws and unscrupulous people. Amelanchier embodies these traits and practices. She knows the truth and refuses to tell it, for even as she is telling it to Elizabeth, she has laced the girl's mug of tea with deadly poison that would bring about Elizabeth's death. For people who have never suffered persecution, this seems an extreme position to take. For people on the inside of the Melungeon story, it makes perfect sense.

Finishing this novel, the reader is left to decide for herself what she thinks. Because McCrumb is taking a shot at what she views as another

---

[25]McCrumb, *Bones*, 205–207.

abuse, the politics of gaining tribal status, no one in the novel really has the luxury of any time to reflect on the moral implications of murder as a justifiable act if it assures survival. Amelanchier only spends twelve hours in jail before a "hot-shot lawyer from Atlanta" who specializes in minority rights is up in the mountains taking her case for free. It is clear that this fictional isolate group, like the Lumbees did in South Carolina, would gain the status they were seeking.

These two novels are very different from each other. In *Hills* McCrumb seems more serious. There are so many layers to the work, so many characters, so many threads, so many stories. Each reader's experience is different depending on which character she chooses to identify with. Any one of the people portrayed would be a good choice. Hamelin, Tennessee, is a "real" place. The time is now. The story is compelling. Sabrina, the Melungeon character, is a minor character until the end of the novel when she is catapulted onto center stage. Her heritage seems to be the reason that she has no internal resources to fall back on. The years of marginalization for Melungeon families in the mountain culture force her into a corner from which she cannot escape.

On the surface, *Lovely in Her Bones* seems light-hearted. There are places in the story that made me laugh out loud as McCrumb takes potshots at Daniel Hunter Coltsfoot, the North Carolina Sherriffs' Association, and hot-shot lawyers who represent persons whose minority rights are being infringed upon. However, simply reading through the list of references to Melungeon history and folklore that I presented above shows that McCrumb takes the isolate group in the novel and their plight very seriously. She is creatively and powerfully using information in the context of a good story. Sarvice Valley also becomes a real place for the reader, and the bitterness of those who inhabit it wreaks havoc for the outsiders—the anthropology team, the FBI, and the local sherriff.

These two novels show how McCrumb uses one Appalacian legend—the Melungeon story—to convey important ideas. In *She Walks These Hills,* Sabrina murders her own child, a terrible crime. However, we as readers can see why she is driven to such an act. She is abandoned by her unfaithful husband, shunned by her in-laws, denied access to education, and left to care for the infant all by herself—she is a de facto captive in Painter Cove. The historical parallel of Katie Wyler reinforces our feelings of sympathy for Sabrina. Persons in extreme circumstances can be driven to bloody deeds. Her behavior seems to be excused or at least explained by the fact of her Melungeon heritage. This behavioral unpredictability is, after all a part of the legend.

Lovely in Her Bones explores another issue entirely. Mixed race peoples, who can demonstrate Native American ancestry, have tried, some successfully and some unsuccessfully, to gain tribal status. In this novel readers see the political system exposed. It seems a foregone conclusion at the end, that because of the political climate, the Cullowhees (thinly disguised Melungeons) will get their tribal status whether they truly deserve it or not. McCrumb explores many typical Melungeon markers. The group of people has no language, no folklore, no music, no crafts. However, Amelanchier Stecoah tells stories that are life experience for people with Melungeon heritage. She describes how the Cullowhees were denied access to medical care, how they were owned by Cherokees, how they tried to hold on to their land. The sherriff adds other details about the onery nature of the men of Sarvice Valley, their tendency to drink, their propensity for breaking the law. In this novel racial and class prejudice of Appalachia is laid bare; it is not a pretty sight.

Like other Appalachian novelists, McCrumb uses Melungeon characters and Melungeon lore to show important truths about the region and being human. She creates for her readers an unforgettable experience in a recognizable place.

The World of Sharyn McCrumb

Mountain Communities Caught within Tradition and Change

Joyce Compton Brown

In her Ballad novels—*If Ever I Return, Pretty Peggy-O, The Hangman's Beautiful Daughter, She Walks These Hills,* the *Rosewood Casket, The Ballad of Frankie Silver,* and *The Songcatcher*—Sharyn McCrumb appears to offer an incongruous mix of the facile and the complex, the "easy read" and the intellectual challenge: one could, with limited consideration of and familiarity with her works, perhaps label her as a "local color" writer, a writer of historical fiction, a mystery novelist, a money-maker for the "mass media" paperback trade. Regardless of the easy labels we as readers might wish to affix to her words and to her, we can see emerging from her early mystery novels to her most recent "ballad novels" a writer whose works carry the theme of inevitable change but inevitable timelessness of the human condition. In particular, she deals with the theme of survival in the face of change—both individual and community, with clear focus on the Appalachian communities she knows and loves. From the earlier mysteries which move from Virginia to North Carolina to Scotland, eventually McCrumb focuses in her Ballad novels on the community of Hamelin, Tennessee, on the North Carolina border, as the prototype of Appalachian community in a state of transition.

In so doing, she defines and confronts major elements threatening survival on both the individual and communal levels, dealing with complex realities of those elements and the complexity of the individuals who struggle to maintain economic, emotional, and spiritual health in today's Appalachia. She combines components of the modern popular genre, mystery fiction, with traditional elements of Appalachian rural culture to call to question the matter of old and new values, of mutability and timelessness. From the loss of the land and a way of life imposed upon Native Americans by settlers to the loss of the land and a way of life imposed upon Appalachian farmers by urbanite vacationers and real estate agents, McCrumb shows the human yearning for home. From the desperate act of a young woman captured by Indians to the desperate act of a young woman captured by ignorance, poverty and abuse, McCrumb shows women through time trapped by biology and cultural servitude. From the haunted lovers of ancient ballads to love letters from Viet Nam, McCrumb presents the endless tragedy and violence of love. Apocalyptic scenes of destruction offer us a new version of Paradise Lost, rivers polluted by paper-mill waste, children destroyed by the bestiality of their fathers, the weakness of their mothers. With increasing technical and thematic sophistication, she has moved toward emergence as an accomplished writer whose works fill the void between shallow romantic stereotyping of the past and flippant dismissal of all tradition. The world of Appalachia, even those aspects of Appalachia that may move beyond the logistics of "rational" explanation, is treated with respect.

Sharyn McCrumb is a masterful weaver of threads of past and present. In her choice of theme and subject, she defines the universality of Appalachia's past and the impact of world events on Appalachia's present. Today's college professor is still pondering the mystery of the death of a young eighteenth-century victim of an Indian massacre while today's sheriff's deputy is still dealing with post Vietnam battle trauma. Today's illegal dumping of polluting waste collides with yesterday's manner of handling grievance against a neighbor, and an unlettered powerless poor mountain man spends his life in prison for confronting his neighbor in the old fashioned individual way.

While the Elizabeth MacPherson novels begin to reveal these later themes and techniques with their use of repeated characters, motifs, and settings, the Ballad novels emerge as increasingly beautifully crafted pictures of today's Appalachian complexity: its community struggles, its communal will to survive, its diverse inhabitants.

Even in *Lovely in Her Bones*, a seemingly "lightweight" mystery novel, McCrumb tackles the question of tribal "isolates" in her portrayal of a Cullowhee community attempting to attain tribal status so that it may survive as an entity with cultural and economy identity. In the Ballad novels, the community of Hamelin, Tennessee, contends with internal and external forces in seeking balance of old and new while under siege by economic difficulties, limited concepts of gender roles and family, outside forces which pollute both its waters and its people, and internal division with regard to the best interests for the future.

With heightened success in the Ballad novels, McCrumb uses opening poems, epigraphs, and internal "outside" texts as sources to link the past and present, as thematic italics. *If Ever I Return, Pretty Peggy-O* utilizes traditional ballads, poems from past and modern times, Thomas Wolfe, and even The Doors to connect the past with the present, using "outside" texts as thematic support in connecting old stories of love, war, and loneliness with the modern story of a woman who does not return the love a young lonely Vietnam soldier and of the continuing scars of the war on the next generation.

In *The Hangman's Beautiful Daughter*, epigraphs from sources both ancient and modern clearly establish the novel's premise of the timelessness of suffering, the cycle of winter death and spring renewal, of inexplicable tragedy and spiritual resilience. The novels' parallel plots present death in the winter: A young boy kills his parents and younger brother and commits suicide as a desperate attempt to stop the cycle of cruelty and abuse perpetrated by his father; an old man returns to retire in his childhood mountain paradise only to learn that his best friend is dying of cancer from the polluting chemicals sent from a morally indifferent North Carolina paper mill into the flowing Tennessee waters of the Little Dove River; a minister's wife tries to serve as a sustaining substitute for

her absent husband, whose Desert Storm ministry seems no more a battle
than her own battle to find hope in the tragic stories around her. Her own
body carries winter death, as she learns that her child is dead within her
womb. A "poor white" mother dies in the effort to save her child from
the flames of their burning trailer. McCrumb sets the tone for these sagas
of death with passages from pre-Christian Britain—"Summer for the
living/Winter for the dead," from Job, from Shakespeare—"A sad tale's
best for winter: I have one/ Of sprites and Goblins," from ballads and
folksongs—"Oh who sits weeping on my grave/ And will not let me
sleep?" and from modernity—"...another outside industry come down
from the hills in the dark for raw material."[1] Yet the epigraphs reinforce
the theme of human hope, of Appalachian resiliency: an old man
commits to activism to clean up a mountain river; a young woman,
losing her own child, becomes mother to a four year old whose own
mother has died; Nora Bonesteel's old groundhog, Persey, awakens to a
new spring. McCrumb's epigraph of hope resounds: "Love lives again,
that with the dead has been:/Love is come again like wheat that springeth
green."[2]

    In *She Walks These Hills*, McCrumb's epigraphs, though still
varied, offer a more specific Appalachian focus. The use of a passage
from James Still's beautiful "Heritage" sets the tone of the book: "One
with the destined feet of man Climbing and descending. And one with
death rising to bloom again, I cannot go. Being of these hills, cannot pass
beyond."

    With the novel's focus on the human need for coming home, she
prefaces chapters with songs such as "Farther Along," and "Steal Away
Home." Other epigraphs speak eloquently of human suffering and faith
in the words of hymns from the *Tennessee Methodist Hymnal* (1885).
When old Harm Sorley escapes from prison and journeys toward home,
he thinks he is a young man making his way back to his wife and
children. Because of a medical condition, which has taken away his more
immediate memory, he is still living in the past, envisioning his return to

---

[1] Sharyn McCrumb, *The Hangman's Beautiful Daughter* (New York: Penguin, 1992) 231.

[2] McCrumb, *Hangman*, 376.

a trailer with a young wife and infant daughter awaiting him. In truth, the trailer has been abandoned for years, and Harm's journey is a journey toward the truth of his lost years. As he nears home, he sees the smoke of the trailer, which is now in flames. In anticipating the end of Harm's illusion, the end of this life, McCrumb uses "After a Fire" from the hymnal, and the words, "When earth and seas and stars and skies,/In flames shall melt away." Hiram's universe does indeed melt away in the fire.

Harm's is not the only journey homeward in *She Walks These Hills*. The ghost of Katie Wyler has been journeying homeward since the eighteenth century; Deputy Joe LeDonne, the troubled Vietnam vet who has trouble confronting his own emotions, finally journeys to a recognition of his love for Martha Ayers; Charlotte Pentland, who has lived her life as the "respectable" stepdaughter of a prosperous unloving businessman, journeys to acceptance of her real origins, the daughter of poor Hiram Sorley and his wife Rita, born into poverty but in a home of love. Others journey homeward in a spiritual sense, toward understanding of themselves and others: A college professor learns that knowledge goes beyond dry facts and finite explanations. A sheriff learns to deal with his own humanity. McCrumb prefaces the closing chapter with the hymn of all hymns included in the *Tennessee Methodist Hymnal*, "Amazing Grace"—"'Tis grace has brought me safe thus far/And grace will lead me home."[3] Reinforcing her emphasis on the loneliness and the uncertain outcome of each journey homeward, McCrumb gives voice to Thomas Wolfe, an Appalachian writer who himself tried to go home. Nora Bonesteel quotes Wolfe: "Which of us is not forever prison-pent... Which of us is not forever a stranger and alone?"[4]

The *Rosewood Casket* is prefaced by Jim Wayne Miller's fine poem, "Small Farms Disappearing in Tennessee." Miller's poem beautifully anticipates the tragedy in McCrumb's story of Dovey Stallard, who is killed trying to save the family farm from being claimed by a real estate agent who would divide and subdivide Appalachia into

---

[3] Sharyn McCrumb, *She Walks These Hills* (New York: Signet, 1994) 427.
[4] McCrumb, *Walks*, 420.

urban neighborhoods with a view. With wonderful use of absurdity to pinpoint the tragic, Miller states, "A number of small Tennessee farms were traced to a land-developer's safe deposit box in a mid-state bank after a bank official entered the vault to investigate roosters crowing and cows bawling inside the box."

To further emphasize her theme that the claiming and reclaiming of land is a timeless cycle seen in the course of Native American history as well as in the present assertion of power, McCrumb begins her saga with Pinero: "I believe the future is simply the past, entered through another gate."[5]

As she tells the story of the present imposing upon traditional Appalachian small farm life, McCrumb extensively uses quotes from Daniel Boone, who was a major figure in opening this Appalachian land to Euro-American settlement at the cost of the Native American way of life in the eighteenth century. Perhaps Boone's most telling comment concerning his own role effecting change and the continuing forced change upon Appalachia prefaces the death of Dovey Stallard, who has accidentally shot the sheriff in a standoff attempt to drive a vulture/real estate agent off her farm: " 'My footsteps,' said Boone, 'have often been marked with blood.'"[6] Yet, in another instance of the end of a family farm, family members try to deal with the last requests of a dying father who wants his death rites handled in a traditional way. McCrumb offers Boone's observation, "It is never too late to Do good [sic]."[7] So that the car salesman son, the country music singer son, the somewhat "hippie" son come together to build a coffin out of old rosewood using hand tools from their father's shop because their father wants them to do so. And wives and lovers (women) gather strips of old cloth to make a quilt for the old man's coffin. And these displaced Appalachians scurry to find a recipe for a "scripture" cake because an old man has asked that his passing be observed in the traditional way.

McCrumb masterfully juxtaposes plots of the past with those of the present, often showing later problems growing out of the seeds of earlier

----

[5] Sharyn McCrumb, *The Rosewood Casket* (New York: Signet, 1996) 11.

[6] McCrumb, *Rosewood*, 376.

[7] McCrumb, *Rosewood*, 132.

unsolved ones. One of her Elizabeth McPherson novels, *If I'd Killed Him When I Met Him*, poses the question of a nineteenth-century woman's murder of her abusive husband against contemporary instances of abused wives. In *She Walks These Hills*, the story of Katie Wyler, captured by Indians in 1779, is juxtaposed with the story of Sabrina Harkryder, a young woman who marries into ignorance, poverty, and abuse, equally captured. Both young women, in their desperation to escape, kill their infant children. In *The Hangman's Beautiful Daughter*, Nora Bonesteel's memories and excursions off the path of time show the mountains in a state of transition, yet constant.

In *The Rosewood Casket*, the old story of a child left to die in a pit contains the seeds of later tragedy. Randall Stargill, as a child, had listened to his murderer-grandmother's instructions to keep silent about his little half sister's being trapped in an isolated pit, where she eventually dies. As a consequence, his own mother never again touches him in love; as a further consequence, he is unable to demonstrate love to his own children, now grown and assimilated into urban America but suffering in varying degrees from emotional crippling. The past haunts the present, McCrumb shows, in the ghost of little Fayre Stargill, still lost in the woods, still seeking a place to belong.

The modern tragedy of Dovey Stallard's loss of her farm and of her life is juxtaposed against the story of Nancy Ward, the Cherokee woman whose peaceful attempts to work with white settlers as a means of saving her tribal land resulted only in her death in 1824 as an old woman, aware that her people would soon be driven from their land. But the dying Nancy Ward predicts the tragedy of Dovey Stallard: "But their time too would pass. She knew that someday the settlers' descendents would lose the land as well. Then they would know the sorrow of leaving a place that was part of you. She wondered what manner of people would come after them."[8]

Through her seer, Nora Bonesteel, McCrumb offers us visions of the past and of the present. In *The Rosewood Casket*, Nora's vision of the spirit of Randall Stargill compels her to convey the bones of his dead little sister to be buried with him in order to resolve old guilts and unrest.

---

[8] McCrumb, *Rosewood*, 27.

In *The Hangman's Beautiful Daughter*, Nora knows Laura Bruce's child will be stillborn, but she knits a sweater for the four-year-old who will become Laura Bruce's adopted son. Nora moves through time so that the readers can see clearly the interconnections of life's past and present. Other examples abound.

Through ghosts and voices of the past who may "pair" with present day characters, McCrumb gives up pictures of individuals and a region haunted by the past. In *The Rosewood Casket*, Dovey Stallard openly identifies with the Cherokee "Beloved Woman" Nancy Ward rather than the meek wifely Rebecca Boone. Clayt Stargill enjoys giving "Daniel Boone" performances at local schools and tries to envision his Appalachia as it was in 1761.[9] In *She Walks These Hills*, a romantic young college professor is forced to recognize the parallels between the eighteenth-century young captive, Katie Wyer, who escapes and runs from her Indian captors, and the "trashy" hillbilly Sabrina Harkryder, who also escapes and runs from entrapment.

While the past holds great power over McCrumb's world and its inhabitants, life with that sense of past is a richer life than a life devoid of a sense of communal history. Rather than resorting to stereotyped "good guy" insider and "bad guy" outsider inhabitants of Wake County, Tennessee, Sharyn McCrumb shows that those with roots may feel compelled or may even choose to sell their past. Thus, in the *Rosewood Casket*, the Stargill farm is split into parcels of real estate to be sold by the brothers who have forfeited their heritage while two other brothers who want to hold on are able to keep their share of the land. Indeed, Frank Whitescarver, the piranha real estate agent in the *Rosewood Casket* who drives around in his Jeep Cherokee looking for family farms to turn into urban developments, is a native of east Tennessee; thus, he knows which families are most vulnerable to his persuasive offers to purchase their land. And *She Walks These Hills* villian Claib Maggard, who makes deals with polluters to dump poisonous chemicals on his neighbor's land, is a respectble local citizen. Those who readily sell their heritage, sell their past, sell their neighbors, appear as Faustian characters whose very souls have been forfeited as a part of the bargain. In contrast, "outsiders,"

[9] McCrumb, *Rosewood,* 54.

such as Laura Bruce, the minister's wife in the *Hangman's Beautiful Daughter*, "Hank the Yank," radio DJ, and Jeremy Cobb, graduate student in *She Walks These Hills*, learn to go beyond simplistic assumptions, develop a sense of the region's past and its connectedness to the present, and grow spiritually as a result of their experiences. Native Appalachians Dovey Stallard (*Rosewood Casket*) and Harm Sorley (*She Walks These Hills*) choose to die rather than live in a world in which they are denied their past.

However, McCrumb offers us a focus on strong Appalachians, men and women who hold to their Appalachian past and recognize that their Appalachian present is no longer safely isolated from the world. As Nora Bonesteel says, "I used to think I was safe from everything up here, being so far removed from civilization, but the world has a way of getting smaller. New York reached out with the chestnut blight and got me, and now the river comes into the valley, bringing the taint with it."[10]

Tavy Annis and Taw McBride, who force the president of the North Carolina paper company that is polluting the Little Dove River to drink a jar of that polluted water recognize the present dangers to their community and have the courage to act even in their old age. Spencer Arrowood, the sheriff trying to deal with the ghost of his "perfect" dead brother; Joe LeDonne, still doing battle with Viet Nam; Martha Ayers, rising from a failed marriage to break down the gender barrier of deputy in a gender-conscious community; Laura Bruce, who sees that "every woman in Dark Hollow [is] exactly one man away from welfare"—these are the new generation of Appalachians working to solve their personal and communal problems in the world of the east Tennessee mountains.

Thus, Sharyn McCrumb brings together in her Ballad novels the themes which she began in the mysteries. With artistic deftness, she offers us an Appalachia besieged by the failures and problems of the world at large—pollution, ethnic and gender prejudice, ethical questions

---

[10] McCrumb, *Hangman*, 378.

regarding the selling of heritage, manipulation of the powerless for economic greed, poverty, corruption, and despair, yet somehow sustained by the hope and courage of those who love her mountains and communities.

The Songcatcher

"Cosmic Possums" on the
Appalachian Song Path

Linda Mills Woolsey

In her afterword to *The Songcatcher*, Sharyn McCrumb aptly describes her novel as "*Roots* with a tune."[1] Like Alex Haley's well-known work, the *Songcatcher* uses the author's own family genealogy to construct the story. It follows the McCourrys from the day Malcolm, the boy who will become its founding father, is kidnapped from his homeland to the moment, more than three centuries later, when his descendent, Lark McCourry (Linda Walker) recovers the lyrics of a ballad that has become the family legacy. That ballad, "The Rowan Stave," is, as McCrumb suggests, "the centerpiece of this novel."[2] More than a structuring motif, in *The Songcatcher* the ballad has become the protagonist. The novel hinges on the fate of that song, more than on the fate of any one character.

---

[1] Sharyn McCrumb, *The Songcatcher* (New York: Signet, 2001) 404.
[2] McCrumb, *Songcatcher,* 402.

In the *Songcatcher*, McCrumb depicts the way a song is "passed on" and the changes that occur as it is reshaped by local language, available instruments, and the musical "ear" of those who transmit it. The ballad McCrumb created for *The Songcatcher* contains a number of the novel's themes: journeys and exile, links between parents and children, connections between the living and dead, and the inevitability of isolation and change. For most of the novel the song is primarily a patriarchal heritage, one nearly lost because Lark, as twelve-year-old Linda Walker, is "banished."[3] from the porch community of singing men. Yet the ballad often connects men and women, from Malcolm teaching it to Rachel in eighteenth-century New Jersey to Spencer Arrowood singing it to Lark in contemporary Tennessee. In the end, this patriarchal heritage is preserved by two women: Nora, who carries the communal memory, and Lark, who carries its songs. "The Rowan Stave" enters the McCourry family narrative when lowlander Robert Bell teaches it to the young highlander Malcolm. The song resonates with Malcolm because "its mournful notes called to [his] mind the songs back home."[4] With the ballad, Bell teaches responsibility toward the song and toward the dead who made it: "When you are given a song that has been handed along from singer to singer over the years, you are entrusted with it, for it is the work of folk who are gone now. Their song. Not yours. It is not your place to change it. You must pass it along to others, and keep it as good as you found it. Sing it as you got it or not at all."[5] Yet *The Songcatcher* ultimately suggests that songs belong to the living and that surface changes in the song are inevitable. Early in the story, Malcolm and Elizabeth "could not find all the right notes" on the pianoforte, and the tune is "changed a bit."[6] Malcolm lets Elizabeth keep the changes, for she is more important to him than the ballad itself. Later, a Dutchman finds the ballad's "Irish" tune difficult. "In truth," Malcolm says, "he never did get the tune quite right, but he seemed to think that his way of playing it improved the song."[7]

---

[3] McCrumb, *Songcatcher,* 23.

[4] McCrumb, *Songcatcher,* 71.

[5] McCrumb, *Songcatcher,* 73–74.

[6] McCrumb, *Songcatcher,* 109.

[7] McCrumb, *Songcatcher,* 177.

Over the years, change is made by both love and arrogance.

As it follows the song, *The Songcatcher* evokes the Ballad novels' recurrent motif of "the chain of serpentine" that forms "a remnant of togetherness" linking the new world and the old, contemporary Appalachia and the timeless mountains.[8] Here, songs and stories give the world a shape and connect human beings to the land, and to one another. Songs are also a "touchstone with the past," a chance to join "a chain of voices stretching all the way back across the ocean, to the place where the families began."[9] This chain is forged in suffering, for, as Malcolm declares, "All of us sing more from sorrow than from joy. It is tragedy that leaves a mark on the mind and calls for the tribute of a song. Happiness is its own gift and needs no other."[10] *The Songcatcher* follows a chain of voices, creating its own "song path" of suffering and change.

Like a number of McCrumb's novels, *The Songcatcher* interweaves two narrative lines, one in the past and one in the present. This time, the historical narrative is a chain of first person accounts. These narratives vividly illustrate McCrumb's sense of the "fragility of one's heritage" while they explore family dynamics that produce three centuries of alienation and discord.[11] The present narrative focuses on the parallel stories of Joe LeDonne and Lark McCourry who find themselves trapped in separate crash sites in the mountain wilderness. As Ben Hawkins and Nora Bonesteel search for Lark's "lifeline"[12] song and as Baird Christopher and Anne McNeill piece together their knowledge of neighbors to locate the "turtle" that is the only clue to the crash's location,[13] the narrative explores what it means to "own" a song or a story and what it means to be at home. The novel depicts a sharp divide between those who want to possess their heritage as a commodity and those willing to belong to that heritage and pass it on.

While the "songcatchers" of the novel's title have made commodities of many old songs, the path to "The Rowan Stave" lies not

---

[8] McCrumb, *Songcatcher,* 157.
[9] McCrumb, *Songcatcher,* 269.
[10] McCrumb, *Songcatcher,* 68.
[11] McCrumb, *Songcatcher,* 404.
[12] McCrumb, *Songcatcher,* 228.
[13] McCrumb, *Songcatcher,* 314.

through their copyrighted manuscripts, but through Nora Bonesteel's genealogical knowledge and insights into the worlds of the living and the dead. Nora sees the ownership embodied in songcatcher copyrights as a delusion, for it is as silly for people to think they can "own a song they didn't write" as it is to try to "buy stars."[14] Even Bonnie Wolfe, who learned the ballad from her family, cannot claim exclusive ownership. Nora tells Bonnie, "A song like that belongs to everybody. Not just to you or your family. That song belongs to all of us and I reckon it is up to the living to keep it going. You can't make it dead just because you are."[15] Like the Appalachian mountains, songs are greater and more enduring than the people who claim them. "Songs," Nora muses, "were like seeds: They wanted to be scattered so that things would grow far from where they started. They didn't care who took them where, or why."[16] Ownership and belonging are also explored in the novel's portraits of "outlanders" and "cosmic possums." Both Joe Le Donne, the "outlander," and Lark McCourry, the "cosmic possum," begin by wondering where they really belong. Le Donne, whose Ohio birthplace is no longer home, heads into the wilderness alone. Lark, estranged from her father, heads back to the mountains out of duty and in the hope of finding a song she can turn into a hit. Ultimately, each of them gains a sense of what it means to be "from around here" in McCrumb's Appalachia.

Whether forced from home by kidnapping or war, or driven by restlessness and yearning, each generation of McCrumb's characters faces the possibility of leaving home and returning to find oneself or the homeland irrevocably changed. At first, it seems that all one can hope for is a survival achieved by renouncing the past. As Malcolm puts it, "In that instant on the beach, I passed out of one life and into another. Later I would realize that I must learn to survive in the new existence, without burdening myself with thoughts of what I left behind."[17]. But survival is not enough. As a human being, Malcolm yearns for home.

---

[14] McCrumb, *Songcatcher,* 269.
[15] McCrumb, *Songcatcher,* 311.
[16] McCrumb, *Songcatcher,* 269.
[17] McCrumb, *Songcatcher,* 46.

He finds that home in the southern Appalachian highlands he comes at last to identify with the legendary "Tir Nan Og"—where the dead go. While Malcolm's family think his dying words refer to turning hawks or hogs,[18] in reality, they signify his deepest homecoming. Even John Walker, who is as alienated from his mountain culture as he is from his daughter Lark/Linda, will find that death, in its proper season, is a "journey...safely home" in the company of those who have died before him.[19]

Yet the novel's primary focus is not on death, but on survival, especially in the face of change. Malcolm avoids his one chance to return to his birthplace, declaring, "I was afraid to see my old home, for fear that the reality would taint my childhood memories."[20] Instead, he chooses a place that reminds him of Scotland, "not the place as it would be now, but the golden country of [his] childhood."[21] Throughout the novel both outlanders and locals feel the pull of the "golden country" of nostalgia, but the true inheritors of McCrumb's Appalachia are those who can adjust to its realities, catching "the tune" of its ways. As they do so, they both preserve the heritage and transform it.

Some of them are true "cosmic possums," a term Sharyn McCrumb and Baird Christopher borrow from Tennessee poet Jane Hicks. "Cosmic possums" were "born to the first generation out of the holler or off the ridge. Grew up in touch with those generations who settled these mountains."[22] As children they learned old customs, old skills, old songs, and old stories, but "did not live in that world."[23] A "cosmic possum" grows up to be a "citizen of the world" who eats "penne pasta" but still knows how to make a "poke salad."[24] "Cosmic possums" live "in the modern world" but they know "what has been lost."[25]

[18] McCrumb, *Songcatcher,* 263.
[19] McCrumb, *Songcatcher,* 28–29.
[20] McCrumb, *Songcatcher,* 91.
[21] McCrumb, *Songcatcher,* 180.
[22] McCrumb, *Songcatcher,* 273.
[23] McCrumb, *Songcatcher,* 273.
[24] McCrumb, *Songcatcher,* 274.
[25] McCrumb, *Songcatcher,* 274.

Of course, some mountain people, like John Walker's housekeeper, Becky Tilden, never stray far or change much. A child of the trailer parks who never finished high school, Becky is also a survivor, though her "greatest skill" is simply the resigned doggedness that enables her to put up with her employer and gradually usurp his daughter's place.[26] Other locals, like Jenna Leigh Gentry, merely contemplate change, toying with the idea of "giving the big city a try."[27] But cosmic possums like Baird Christopher are just as much "locals" as Becky and Jenna Leigh. While Baird makes jaunts to Ecuador and New Zealand, he is anchored firmly in his mountain home.

"Cosmic possums" like Baird, Arrowood, and Lark rub shoulders with two kinds of "outlanders: those who, like Malcolm, find "the tune" of the mountains and make it their adopted home and those who, like the "corporate guy" on Lark's bus "didn't get it"— the gawking tourists and predatory songcatchers who come to consume and exploit Appalachia.[28] While not all outlanders are pushy "Eastern urbanites" or "arrogant tourists,"[29] even the most well-meaning bring change: "The new people professed to want simple country living, but soon they found that they also wanted portobello mushrooms, the *Wall Street Journal,* computer technicians, nouvelle cuisine, and a wine shop."[30] The "locals" themselves are changing. Spencer Arrowood, uneasy in outlander-ridden Bluff Mountain,[31] orders spinach salads, and sniffs at iceberg lettuce as "rabbit fodder"—an opinion that earns him the sobriquet of "cosmic possum" from a waiter at the "French Broad Bistro."[32] Having been to the service and to school, Arrowood is as changed as the travelers of the "The Rowan Stave" ballad.

Just as locals are changed by their experiences of the outland world, outlanders like Ben Hawkins are changed by the mountains. Ben came from New Jersey for a visit, found a vocation in pottery, and like

---

[26] McCrumb, *Songcatcher,* 7.
[27] McCrumb, *Songcatcher,* 144.
[28] McCrumb, *Songcatcher,* 18.
[29] McCrumb, *Songcatcher,* 158-59.
[30] McCrumb, *Songcatcher,* 162.
[31] McCrumb, *Songcatcher,* 161.
[32] McCrumb, *Songcatcher,* 152.

Malcolm, "never did go home."[33] When he comes to ask Nora Bonesteel's help in tracking down the ballad, Ben brings a gift of a handmade pot to avoid being "beholden." Although he is "one of the new people," she sees that "his instincts [are] good," and knows "He would fit in well."[34] Here McCrumb pictures Appalachian culture as a living entity, shaped by those who come to the mountain today, as it has been by many others during its long history. In this, her Appalachia mirrors the reality of a United States formed and still being formed by its restless, changing people.

The "songcatchers" represent a darker side of the "outlanders." The term "songcatcher" was coined by the mountain people to describe the musicologists who came to seeking songs to record.[35] The songcatcher in Ellender McCourry's narrative defines his work as "searching for a piece of the past that has been lost where I come from."[36] Most outlanders, like Jamie Raeburn, see the work of the songcatchers as a good thing, a way of "Preserving the heritage."[37] But Lark realizes that "Nothing is ever that easy."[38]

Nora Bonesteel links songcatchers with other outlanders who try to cheat mountain people because they think "we wouldn't know any better."[39] Some professional songcatchers, like their amateur sisters--the patronizing tourist ladies who don't recognize Zeb's quote from Shakespeare— enact a disdain for the very mountain culture they are consuming.[40] As Zeb discovers, sometimes would-be "benefactors" are not friends.[41] While the songcatchers preserve songs, they do so by making them marketable commodities, copyrighting songs they didn't write. Virgil Swift likens this to "intellectual strip mining"[42] and song

---

[33] McCrumb, *Songcatcher*, 190.

[34] McCrumb, *Songcatcher*, 239.

[35] McCrumb, *Songcatcher*, 352.

[36] McCrumb, *Songcatcher*, 352.

[37] McCrumb, *Songcatcher*, 23.

[38] McCrumb, *Songcatcher*, 23.

[39] McCrumb, *Songcatcher*, 213.

[40] McCrumb, *Songcatcher*, 329.

[41] McCrumb, *Songcatcher*, 357.

[42] McCrumb, *Songcatcher*, 279.

"rustling."[43] Bonnie Wolfe sees it as a racket: "Imagine that—you get a song for free on the pretense of preserving it for posterity, and then you go and put your name on it and charge people to sing it."[44] Yet outlanders are not the only would-be predators. Though scornful of the songcatchers, Bonnie herself wants exclusive ownership of the ballad.[45]

As a singer-songwriter whose own first hit, "Prayers the Devil Answers" was drawn from family lore, Lark finds herself caught between the world where music is business and "everything is image" and the world where music is the sorrowing language of real people.[46] Lark, who has "made a musician" much as her father "made a lawyer" echoes the pride in achievement that Benjamin McCourry brought to his father's wake generations before.[47] Like Benjamin, arriving too late, she fails to find blessing or apology. But while Benjamin rejects the legacy of "The Rowan Stave," Lark embraces it. In doing so, she literally and figuratively breaks free from the false values and harbored resentment that entrap her.

Musing on connections between shelling peas and butterflies escaping their cocoons, Baird Christopher provides an image for this liberation: *"They know what its like to be inside a pod, only no one helps them break out. They have to do it on their own.* Now with people, some folks break out of their own pods, and some have to be broken out by others, but it doesn't matter which way you are set free. The important thing is that you emerge—get out there into the great world and seek your destiny."[48] For both Joe Le Donne and Lark McCourry breaking out is also going home.

The solitary birthday hike that leads to Joe Le Donne's entrapment, begins with his declaring "I want to go home."[49] A war-scarred outlander ill at ease in his adopted Wake County, Le Donne has neither "family

[43] McCrumb, *Songcatcher,* 280.
[44] McCrumb, *Songcatcher,* 213.
[45] McCrumb, *Songcatcher,* 214.
[46] McCrumb, *Songcatcher,* 22.
[47] McCrumb, *Songcatcher,* 18–19.
[48] McCrumb, *Songcatcher,* 155.
[49] McCrumb, *Songcatcher,* 53.

connections" nor "church membership."[50] He only feels at home on the trail, where "he would not have to pretend that he belonged."[51] Le Donne connects with the "mountain home" at a deep, inchoate, and cosmic level: "Mountain vistas gave him [...] a sense of being in the presence of an all-encompassing being, and feeling its benevolence toward him."[52] Yet the mountain home is also a dangerous place our technologies only give us the illusion of taming. As Le Donne's and Lark's stories unfold, they reinforce the need to take the wilderness seriously. Even Le Donne's rescuer, Rattler, though steeped in all the old ways, chides him for going off into the wilderness without his cell phone.[53]

At the same time, McCrumb's characters also learn to take life and human relationships seriously. As Le Donne's ordeal nears its close, he finds that it is worth anything to stay alive[54] and wishes he could leave a message for Martha.[55] While Le Donne breaks through some of his scarred shell, Benjamin McCourry fails to escape his early version of the Eastern urbanite curse. Rejecting Malcolm's song, Benjamin imagines his own children as "rooted in the church of their forefathers, and rich in heritage and community."[56] Like others who will come to this "benighted hill country," Benjamin cannot imagine a legacy not measured in titles, achievements, and acres.[57] For much of the novel, Lark seems more than a little trapped by a similar set of values, banking, like Bonnie Wolfe, on her fame.

For Lark, recovering the Rowan ballad becomes a means of bridging the gap between her past and her present, herself and her father. The song does this not through effecting reconciliation, but by enabling her to "remember some of the good times."[58] The song cannot repair the rifts made by gender bias and the family curse, but it remains when the

---

50 McCrumb, *Songcatcher,* 54.
51 McCrumb, *Songcatcher,* 54.
52 McCrumb, *Songcatcher,* 117.
53 McCrumb, *Songcatcher,* 343.
54 McCrumb, *Songcatcher,* 394.
55 McCrumb, *Songcatcher,* 316.
56 McCrumb, *Songcatcher,* 259.
57 McCrumb, *Songcatcher,* 253.
58 McCrumb, *Songcatcher,* 229.

"snapshots faded and the love was lost."[59] "It wasn't," Lark reflects, "a happy song, but she had dredged it up from a better time, maybe the last good time there had ever been between her and her father."[60]

Song and story, memory and connection are at the heart of *The Songcatcher*. Like Lark, McCrumb functions as a sort of "cultural ambassador for Appalachia"[61] out to inform "city types" that "*The Dukes of Hazard* was not a documentary."[62] Both the novelist and her central characters explore what it means to be "from around here." rooted in a sense of kinship, a sense of place, a shared culture.[63] The planes, which carry people in and out, are emblems of mobility and freedom, but also a means of entrapment and mortality as the novel links the downed planes that trap Lark and Le Donne with the crashes that killed Patsy Cline and Bonnie Wolfe.

The quest for home is finally as important as the song quest in the novel. You can be born in a place and feel estranged from it, come from afar and belong. Cosmic possums, outlanders, and folks "from around here" all need a homeland, a human community, and the freedom to live authentically. Like the ballad, McCrumb's Appalachia belongs to those who feel for it, respect, and cherish it. They keep it in trust for those who come after, not unchanged, but with its heart intact. With this, *The Songcatcher* expresses a hope that though it may be changed, something of the mountain culture will survive against the odds, like the "Rowan Stave" ballad so nearly lost.

---

[59] McCrumb, *Songcatcher*, 229.
[60] McCrumb, *Songcatcher*, 229.
[61] McCrumb, *Songcatcher*, 22.
[62] McCrumb, *Songcatcher*, 22.
[63] McCrumb, *Songcatcher*, 203–204.

The Past as Present

Ghosts of the Past in Sharyn McCrumb's Ghost Riders

Kimberley M. Holloway

In the prologue to *The Rosewood Casket*[1] Sharyn McCrumb uses for her opening epigraph a quote from Pinero: "I believe the future is simply the past, entered through another gate." Indeed when she writes or speaks of her craft, McCrumb often remembers of the bedtime stories her father told her. He told her stories like the *Iliad* and the *Odyssey* and old family stories of circuit-riding preachers and the Civil War, ancient stories and not so ancient ones. From this legacy of storytelling, the young listener grew up to tell her own stories in which she, like the storytellers of her childhood, continues to look to the past to interpret the present. Like McCrumb herself, some of the characters in her novels often exhibit a keenly developed sense of the past and its influence on the present. But whether the inhabitants of her fictional Hamelin, Tennessee, realize it or

---

[1] Sharyn McCrumb, *The Rosewood Casket* (New York: Dutton, 1996).

not, the past is a powerful force in their lives. And so it is that in her most recent novel, the past takes center stage.

In the author's note to this novel, *Ghost Riders,* Sharyn McCrumb writes, "I thought that it was worth reminding people that war sometimes seems to take on a life of its own and that hatred has a half-life."[2] Those words effectively sum up the novel itself. First, the novel, which takes place as much in the past as it does in the present, illustrates the awful division that occurred in Appalachian mountain families during the Civil War. But the most intriguing part of that statement is that "hatred has a half-life." In *Ghost Riders*, more than any of the other Ballad novels, McCrumb examines this idea that the past affects the future and that maybe it's best not to dwell on and romanticize the past. For if past troubles encroach on the present, the result might be unpredictable. Some of the characters in this novel soon discover that the leftover bitterness and hatred and divisiveness of that war may somehow still exist in these mountains, smoldering—waiting to exert its influence on the present.

This idea of the past's continuing impact on the present has always been a part of McCrumb's Ballad novels to some extent. In some of these novels the past exerts a more subtle influence, one that characters and readers alike are aware of, almost acutely so at times, but that doesn't always directly bear on events that occur in the present. But in the later Ballad novels, like *The Ballad of Frankie Silver,*[3] *The Songcatcher,*[4] and *Ghost Riders*, the past finally catches up with the present in a very real and tangible way. In each of these three novels, McCrumb has increasingly depicted just how strong that connection between the past and the present can be.

In *The Ballad of Frankie Silver*, uncovering the story of Frankie's crime, trial, and punishment becomes the key to Spencer Arrowood's unraveling of the circumstances of Fate Harkryder's eerily similar case.

---

[2] At the time of this writing *Ghost Riders* had not yet been published, and the title was not yet confirmed. Because the novel was not yet in print, this essay deals only with the larger issue of the impact of the past on the present as depicted in the novel. Except for the quote from the Author's Note, no direct quotes or page numbers are provided, though specific events in the novel are discussed.

[3] Sharyn McCrumb, *The Ballad of Frankie Silver* (New York: Dutton, 1998).

[4] Sharyn McCrumb, *The Songcatcher* (New York: Signet, 2001).

Only when Spencer is able to understand the details of Frankie's story is he able to see the truth of Fate's situation. Though the past and the present are presented as distinctly separate stories held together by Spencer's search for the truth in both cases, the past does have a direct influence on the present.

In *The Songcatcher,* too, Lark McCourry's story is dependent on events of the past. In this novel the journey of the ballad that Lark seeks *seems* to be a separate narrative, but McCrumb's readers sense that she will gradually blend that story line with Lark's own present-day journey to form one seamless narrative. As the story of the lost ballad "The Rowan Stave" progresses from eighteenth-century Scotland through time and distance to present-day Appalachia, so too does Lark's journey lead her to find not just the ballad itself but a sense of the past as well.

But it is in *Ghost Riders* that McCrumb's skill in weaving together events of the past and events of the present into one intricate narrative becomes even more evident than in the previous Ballad novels. This novel demonstrates McCrumb's belief that the past holds a great deal of significance in the present, whether we are aware of it or not. For some characters in Wake County, like Old Rattler and Nora Bonesteel, Spencer Arrowood, and Tom Gentry, the past becomes a more relevant part of their lives than they ever considered possible. Each of these characters must face the past as a part of the present, and they learn as the novel progresses that it is usually best to leave the past in the past.

In *Ghost Riders*, there is a distinct blurring of time. The boundary between the past and the present, between the east Tennessee mountains of the twenty-first century and the east Tennessee mountains of the Civil War, becomes almost indistinguishable. For those who remain unrecptive to the lessons of the past, it is as if the two times are just as removed from each other as they have always seemed to be. The Civil War re-enactors seem to be particularly unaware of the "danger" of not letting the past stay in the past. In their single-minded drive to reproduce the past as accurately as possible in present day Hamelin, Tennessee, they miss the important lessons of the past, that the Civil War was more than just a part of the ever more distant past. It is still here, and its dangers still exist. Because this war tore apart families and friendships, its influence seems never to end, reaching all the way into twenty-first-century Appalachia, bringing the dead soldiers, the ghost riders, with it.

Nora Bonesteel and Old Rattler have seen these ghost riders before and know that it is best to keep one's distance from them. Tom Gentry, though seeking to leave everybody and everything behind him, gets a glimpse of them and discovers just what happens when one does comes face-to-face with the past. While most everyone in the area is unaware of the presence of these riders from the past, these three see and experience the power of the past.

Rattler, who like Nora Bonesteel has the Second Sight, first encounters the past as a genuine danger while he was still a boy. His early encounter with the ghost riders, who are not really dead or alive, has given him a healthy respect for these riders of the past, for he comes to realize that the past still impacts the present, and the negative feelings from this encounter endure throughout Rattler's childhood. Rattler doesn't relish the activities of the Civil War re-enactors who occasionally show up near his home in Wake County, Tennessee. He knows that the war is still being fought in his mountains, and he wishes they would leave the past alone. He sees no good in dredging up the awful pain and conflicts of the Civil War.

When as an adult Rattler encounters a mysterious character known as Ravenmocker, who seems almost omniscient, he learns that the re-enactors are acting as decoys, attracting the long-dead soldiers to the present time and place. Ravenmocker tells Rattler that these solders are using the weapons of their own time and place in present-day Wake County, and that killing is not the point. Later, in a conversation with a neighbor, Rattler discusses the theories of an English physicist who believes that every moment in time lasts forever, that time is not linear but a collection of separate present moments that each continue to exist forever. With the insight that he has gained in these two encounters, Rattler comes to understand the dangers that are imminent in Wake County.

Ultimately, it is Rattler who must save those in this own time who do not understand the potency of a past that will not stay in the past. Rattler himself warns Jeff McCullough, a recurring character in the Ballad novels and in this novel a Civil War re-enactor, not to continue with the re-enactment, that the war is not really over and there is a strong possibility that the hostilities of the past will begin all over again if they do continue. And it is Rattler who explains to Jeff McCullough that magic is found in the old quilts that are still found in most of the homes in Hamelin. He knows that in their ancient patterns, which traveled across the Atlantic from Ireland, there resides the "magic" of family and tradition that can keep people safe—even from the dangers of a dark and powerful past.

Another character who tries to understand the past and the present is Spencer Arrowood. At a visit to the re-enactors' encampment, Spencer is told that one of his ancestors was the last man killed in the Civil War east of the Mississippi in the last battle of the war, the Battle of Waynesville. Because of what he is told, Spencer becomes almost obsessed with the past—with the Civil War—in his search for answers to this question from his own family's past. In a quest to find out if what he has heard is true, Spencer looks in all possible places to find an answer to his questions. While researching the war at the library at East Tennessee State University in nearby Johnson City, Tennessee, he reads accounts of the war and searches rosters listing the various regiments from the area. Finding no answers there, Spencer realizes that he must go back to the past—or at least a battleground from the past—to find the answer to his question. But what he finds when he visits Waynesville is not an answer, only more questions. The battlefield where his ancestor died is not a war memorial as he had expected but a development of middle class homes. The past, in effect, has been buried at this battleground and with it, the answers for which he is searching. Just as Rattler has warned, the Civil War re-enactors have dredged up the past, only to cause more problems. Spencer leaves the "battleground" with no answers and the feeling that he just might not be who he thought he was.

A final character who encounters the past in the present is Tom Gentry, who even more than Rattler and Nora, discovers that the past is a much more powerful force in the southern mountains than most people believe. Tom has turned his back completely on life. He has come to the Appalachian mountains to die, armed with a journal, a tent, and little else. As Gentry slips further and further away from the land of life and the living and toward death, he encounters the ghost riders of the Civil

War in the shadow world between life and death, a liminal place that he has entered as a prelude to his own death.

Liminality is a recurring motif in McCrumb's novels, and *Ghost Riders* is no exception. Rattler, Nora, and Tom Gentry are all liminal characters in one way or another. Liminality is that state of being betwixt and between two things—day and night, heaven and earth, life and death. Because Nora and Rattler have the gift of the Second Sight and can see into the world of the dead, they are often caught between these two worlds. They have seen the ghost riders before and know their significance and the danger they hold for the living. But Tom Gentry is only able to reach that state of liminality as he slips from this world of the living into the world of the dead, a world inhabited by the Civil War soldiers who continue to fight the war even after more than a century and a half.

Ultimately, in the end, the past and the present do blend seamlessly together for a brief moment one night in the Appalachian mountains. And this is only right, for the mountains themselves are liminal—betwixt and between the heavens and the earth. In this novel the lines delineating time and existence in the mountains near Hamelin become so intertwined that the past and the present collide. Those characters, like Rattler, Nora, Jeff McCullough and the group of fiddlers who stay with him at the encampment, who understand and respect that the past retains an element of magic remain safe that night. Others, like Tom Gentry, embrace the past, but in the process, they must cross the temporal boundaries between the past and the present and between life and death, never to return.

The result of this temporal collision in the Tennessee mountains is that some characters gain a fuller understanding of the past and its influence on the present and the future. Unfortunately, however, there are those who remain unknowing or uncaring of the dangers they so carelessly ignore. They will continue to dredge up a romanticized version of the past. And there are those, like Spencer, who will seek for answers but find them elusive, buried forever in the past.

Bibliography of
Sharyn McCrumb's Fiction

The Songcatcher. New York: Dutton, 2001

The Ballad of Frankie Silver. New York: Dutton, 1998.

Bimbos of the Death Sun. New York: Ballantine, 1998.

Foggy Mountain Breakdown and Other Stories. New York: Ballantine, 1997.

Ghost Riders. New York: Dutton, 2003.

The Hangman's Beautiful Daughter. New York: Scribner's 1992.

Highland Laddie Gone. New York: Avon, 1996.

If Ever I Return, Pretty Peggy-O. New York: Scribner's, 1990.

If I'd Killed Him When I Met Him. *New York: Ballantine, 1995.*

Lovely in Her Bones. *New York: Avon, 1985.*

MacPherson's Lament. New York: Ballantine, 1992.

Missing Susan. New York: Ballantine, 1991.

Paying the Piper. New York: Ballantine, 1988.

The PMS Outlaws. New York: Ballantine, 2000.

The Rosewood Casket. New York: Dutton, 1996.

She Walks These Hills. New York: Scribner's, 1994.

Sick of Shadows. New York: Avon, 1984.

The Windsor Knot. New York: Ballantine, 1990.

Zombies of the Gene Pool. New York: Ballantine, 1992.

Index